D0209392

May 2015

i am because you are

How the Spirit of *Ubuntu* Inspired an Unlikely Friendship and Transformed a Community

Jacob Lief

with Andrea Thompson

Foreword by Archbishop Desmond Tutu

RODALE.

ISBN 978–1–62336–449–6   hardcover
ISBN 978–1–62336–661–2   paperback

Distributed to the trade by Macmillan

2   4   6   8   10   9   7   5   3   1   hardcover
2   4   6   8   10   9   7   5   3   1   paperback

To my boys, Madiba and Freedom, for whom a better world awaits, and to Lindsay, who is the reason that I have made it this far. —J. L.

To Mike and Ocie. —A. T.

CONTENTS

FOREWORD

I FIRST MET JACOB LIEF IN JANUARY OF 2006. HE BOUNDED INTO THE lobby of my New York hotel, a young man with long, curly blond hair, an infectious smile, and a palpable passion for South Africa and for his organization, Ubuntu Education Fund. His energy took over the room. The first question I asked him was: "What is a young, white American like you doing in the townships?"

He answered, in the unembellished, undaunted way that I now recognize as his trademark style, "I'm trying to give the kids there the same kind of education you and I would give our own children."

Jacob went on to tell me the story of how he and his partner, Malizole "Banks" Gwaxula, began this important work. They met by chance one night in Port Elizabeth, South Africa; at the time, Jacob was still a college student, while Banks worked full-time as a teacher. After a few hours of conversation, Banks offered Jacob a place to stay and work at his school. They discovered a shared sense of purpose: to improve the lives and education of children living in the townships of Port Elizabeth. Together, they had very little to start with, but they poured themselves into canvasing the community to discover what its residents needed and wanted the most. They set out to gather donations, and their ambitious vision for changing lives inspired enormous generosity.

Soon, Jacob and Banks were providing schools with textbooks, basic supplies, and computer centers. It didn't take long, however, for the pair to realize that raw materials weren't enough, and so they went about creating a support system that encouraged and enabled children to *use* their new resources. Later, when the community sought help in dealing with the pernicious effects of the AIDS crisis, Jacob and Banks responded with health programs and counseling. On that winter afternoon, as I listened to Jacob describe what Ubuntu Education Fund had done so far, and how much more it hoped to accomplish, I realized that it was truly embodying what its name set forth: *Ubuntu* is the recognition of humanity in one another.

This is not just a nice thought or a sentimental set of words in South Africa. Ubuntu is our defining concept: *I* exist because *you* exist. And here was Jacob, telling me how he, as a student at the University of Pennsylvania, met Banks, a black South African some twenty years older, and a teacher in the townships, and how they proceeded to look beyond their superficial differences to their essential sameness. And more than that, they looked beyond their own needs and comforts and saw the needs and discomforts of the people who surrounded them.

South Africa cast off an oppressive regime in favor of a democratic society, and it did so without war. The reconciliation process that followed continues to inspire oppressed people across the globe. And yet the inequities of apartheid linger. A particularly harmful aspect of that legacy is an educational system that lags far behind our capabilities. The Bantu Education Act of 1953 established policies based on the idea that some children neither need nor deserve an education, that reading, writing, and arithmetic are wasted on someone destined to dig a ditch. Because of these policies, township schools sank into a state of disrepair and laxity too great to easily overcome. But, unlike so many before him, Jacob was able to see a hunger to learn in our children—children who crowded three to a desk, even if they had no pens or paper or chalk to write on their classroom blackboards. Through Ubuntu Education Fund, Jacob and Banks sought to relieve that hunger, to bring the sustenance of education to a generation of children.

Jacob and Banks also recognized that a child needs more than books and pencils to succeed at learning. A child must feel safe, must be supported, must be healthy and eat well. As the AIDS epidemic spread in our country, we watched the virus's acute impact on children. Many were HIV-positive and struggling with its symptoms. Others were supporting their families because their mothers or fathers were sick and could not. Still others had no parents at all, left orphaned by the disease.

For several years, the important work of dealing with the effects of HIV/AIDS became derailed by politics. Some wanted to argue about its causes, argue over what remedies were most effective and how the epidemic might be staunched. Meanwhile, thousands of children were being caught up by illness and death. They were being asked to grow up before their time, to become caregivers when they themselves needed care. Throughout this time, as the government failed to resolve these issues, Jacob and his colleagues steadfastly offered support and advocacy to those in need. Their work remains important. There is nothing so tragic as seeing a child stripped of his or her childhood. Ubuntu Education Fund helps children reclaim some of the freedom and the joy that comes from knowing that you have someone to rely on, to help you face the difficult tasks, to listen to your deepest fears, to share in the pleasure of learning, and to revel in the delight of play.

While Ubuntu Education Fund offers children great resources and intensive intervention, perhaps more crucially it teaches children that they deserve the same quality of attention and supplies as anyone else. Defeatism may be one of the most insidious by-products of poverty. If you expect that nothing good will come of your life, why reach for anything better? By bolstering the self-esteem, the confidence, and the self-awareness of children in the townships, Ubuntu Education Fund gives them the tools to work hard, to dream large, and to expect great things to happen.

At that January meeting, Jacob convinced me to speak at Ubuntu's first gala to be held in New York City. Soon after, I became the organization's patron, and over the years, I've spoken at many of its functions, both in London and in New York. I've watched it grow from a handful of people working hard to stretch a few thousand dollars to an organization that, in September 2010, opened a state-of-the-art $6.5-million

community center. The first generation of students has now graduated from university. In turn, Ubuntu has been recognized around the
world. Jacob is a fellow of the Aspen Institute's African Leadership Initiative and has been named a Young Global Leader by the World Economic Forum. The organization has been recognized by the Schwab
Foundation Social Entrepreneur of the Year Award and has often been
highlighted at the Clinton Global Initiative.

After the many years we struggled to rid our country of apartheid,
nothing makes me prouder now than to see South Africa give birth to
organizations like Ubuntu Education Fund, whose work illuminates
the vast difference between simply touching a child's life and truly
transforming it. Ubuntu draws deeply from its community, and the
community draws deeply from it; they have formed a relationship that
beautifully demonstrates how we all depend on each other to thrive.
Through it, we can envision a future when every child believes he or
she deserves the best, and reaches for it.

Look at the origins of Ubuntu: Jacob didn't arrive in Port Elizabeth with the attitude that he knew all the solutions to its problems or
with notions of a quick fix. He came with a humble spirit, with curios-
ity and compassion, with a desire to learn from the people he chose to
serve. He met Banks, who demonstrated the spirit of *ubuntu* by inviting
this young stranger into his home and into his family, and joined him in
a working partnership that depends on respect and trust. In this way,
the seeds of Ubuntu Education Fund were planted, and now they have
borne fruit.

—Archbishop Desmond Tutu

Ubuntu is very difficult to render into a Western language. It speaks of the very essence of being human. When we want to give high praise to someone we say, "Yu, u nobuntu"; "Hey, so-and-so has ubuntu." Then you are generous, you are hospitable, you are friendly and caring and compassionate. You share what you have. It is to say, "My humanity is caught up, is inextricably bound up, in yours." We belong in a bundle of life. We say, "A person is a person through other persons." It is not, "I think therefore I am." It says rather: "I am human because I belong. I participate, I share." A person with ubuntu is open and available to others, affirming of others, does not feel threatened that others are able and good, for he or she has a proper self-assurance that comes from knowing that he or she belongs in a greater whole and is diminished when others are humiliated or diminished, when others are tortured or oppressed, or treated as if they were less than who they are.

—Archbishop Desmond Tutu
No Future without Forgiveness

CHAPTER ONE

The Meaning of a Dress

IN MANY WAYS, ZETHU NGCEZA WAS LIKE ANY OTHER KID IN THE TOWN-ships of Port Elizabeth. Her family struggled to make ends meet—her father was a municipal worker, and her mother was unemployed. They lived together in what was once a men's hostel for migrant workers, sharing the small space with other families. Still, they were a happy family, and laughter filled their home. Then, in 2004, her father died three months after coming down with an HIV-related illness. The following year, her mother fell sick, also with an HIV-related illness, and died after only two months. Zethu's life turned upside-down.

At fourteen, Zethu became the head of her household, taking care of her younger brother, Star, and sister, Lungi. "I started asking myself some questions," she later recalled. "Questions like 'What am

I supposed to do? Should I just go? Should I just run away? I've got dreams. How can I face this thing?' But I told myself, 'These are my siblings. This is my brother, this is my sister. They deserve the best.'"

For a few years, Zethu had been participating in programs that Ubuntu Education Fund ran in her school. She'd grown to trust Zuki, one of the health educators who worked there, and so she confided to her that she and her siblings had been orphaned. Zuki quickly acted. Fezeka, an Ubuntu household stability counselor, visited Zethu's home and figured out what the three children needed immediately. Of most concern was the safety of their home. Burglar bars on the windows, a better door, and a sturdy lock went on the checklist. She brought them a food parcel, with fresh vegetables and pantry staples. They needed better light so they could study, and new uniforms. She assured Zethu that her school fees would be paid.

Zethu wrestled with feelings of anger and guilt, along with her grief. Why was she left alone to take care of her siblings? How could she be a mother to them when she was their sister? Small and slight, she hardly seemed strong enough to carry the responsibility.

Yet, she did. And when she felt overwhelmed or anxious or afraid, she called Fezeka. If they'd run out of cooking oil, or her sister's skirt was too small, or her brother had begun acting out in school, she'd come to Ubuntu for help. And, sometimes, she'd come to Ubuntu to forget all her responsibilities for an hour or two and just be a kid.

~~~~~~~

I first went to South Africa when I was in high school, and I fell in love with the country as soon as I walked off the plane. It was 1994, in the midst of the turbulent transition from apartheid to democracy. The energy, the pride, and the promise of the New South Africa inspired me. When I returned as a student at the University of Pennsylvania, I met Banks Gwaxula, a schoolteacher with an ebullient personality who offered me a place to stay and helped me find work in the townships.

He changed my life. I lived with him for three transformative months, and by the end, I knew what I wanted to do: be a part of the New South Africa. The banter on the street, the smells of red earth and burning coal, the energy of the people, the overpowering congestion inside the urban townships, and the enormous space outside of them—it's intoxicating and invigorating. There's a lawlessness that can be terrifying, and of course has had negative consequences, but also imparts a sense of freedom. The country and the continent have something that goes deep inside, that's inescapable. No matter how far you travel, as they say, the dust of Africa stays on the soles of your feet.

With their extreme poverty and organized chaos, the townships, it seems, shouldn't function. But they do. I was drawn to the people's absolute determination to make good on all of the promises of the anti-apartheid movement. Banks and I decided—with the best intentions but remarkable naïveté—that we wanted to help children achieve their dreams. We didn't know the rules of development; we didn't care about the external measures of success. And we didn't see ourselves as saving anyone. We simply wanted to help create a level playing field for the children we knew in the townships, and we believed that if we could do that, there was nothing they couldn't achieve.

As our organization grew, we realized that what so many of these children really needed was a parent. Whether their own parents were gone or unable to take care of them—because of poverty, HIV, or mental illness—having someone to provide the basics of life was the missing piece. They needed someone to give them anything and everything they needed, like any parents would if they could. After all, hours of tutoring or a health education class meant little when rain leaked through the roof and there was nothing to eat for dinner. For me, Zethu embodied this truth. When I first met her, I couldn't believe how much this tiny girl had to bear each day. Even with Ubuntu's help, life wasn't easy—she had to find time to study, to clean her own and her siblings' clothes, to cook, to help them with their problems. Zethu faced each day as a feat of endurance. And it was immediately apparent just how vulnerable she and her siblings were: They had nothing to fall back on, no safe harbor if something went wrong.

I grew to realize over the years that Zethu and her siblings, in many ways, embodied the struggles all of Ubuntu's clients faced, and their outcomes showed both the triumphs and the challenges that go into trying to intervene in a meaningful way. Not every child will go on to university or a career; sometimes the forces of mental illness or peer pressure or the growing pains of being an adolescent throw up road-blocks. Sometimes they are insurmountable. But in Zethu, Lungi, and Star, I see every child that Ubuntu works with and for—every one who has achieved more than she ever thought possible, and every one that fell along the way.

~~~~~~

In 2006, the Clinton Global Initiative (CGI) asked to meet some of our children who had been orphaned and left to take care of siblings. We arranged an afternoon for forty of these clients to sit in our courtyard with representatives from CGI and tell them about their lives. Zethu sat among the group. The representatives were taken with her vibrant smile and calm confidence, as well as her dedication to her siblings. After a visit to her home, they invited her to speak at their midyear meeting in New York. She delivered a captivating speech to a roomful of influential thinkers, nonprofit leaders, and philanthropists, and charmed former President Bill Clinton with her precocious poise. It was a heady experience. When she came home, it was difficult to return to life as usual: school, caring for Star and Lungi, studying at night. She began to skip classes, run around with boys—act, for once, like a sixteen-year-old.

Those of us at Ubuntu felt the same way any parent dealing with any teenager would feel: exasperated and exhausted. There's a limit to what you can do to curb self-destructive behavior, and to a certain extent, being present and loving is the best you can do. Everyone at Ubuntu cared deeply for this family, and Fezeka wasn't the only one who reached out. Eventually, Zethu realized that she needed to put herself back on track. She rededicated herself to school, came back to Ubuntu for extra help in the afternoons, and started to think about university.

We all celebrated with Zethu when she started her studies in managed accounting at Nelson Mandela Metropolitan University. And as she approached her final exams, we held our breath: She was so close to a diploma, one tangible marker of success.

~~~~~~~

Finally, the moment arrived. Zethu checked her scores with a knot in her stomach. One after another, she read the results: Passed. The relief swept over her. She was going to graduate.

In the back of her mind, underneath the relief and excitement, there was a small kernel of sadness. With graduation came the graduation ceremony. To participate, you had to buy a gown, and most students' parents treated it like a special occasion, with a new dress, a trip to the hair salon, nice shoes. But Zethu didn't have a mother or father to take her shopping, and she knew she didn't have the money. She resigned herself to reality: She would be content with knowing all she had achieved, and leave the celebratory trappings to others.

Her first call was to Fezeka. "I've passed!" Zethu told her. "I'm going to graduate, can you believe it?" Over the years, Fezeka had watched Zethu struggle, fail, pick herself back up, and go back to work. Over all these years, Zethu never acted entitled or grasping; she accepted help with grace, but she often held back from asking for more. Fezeka knew what went into graduation: the hair, the nails, the clothes. But she also knew that Zethu was conscious of all the ways in which she was more fortunate than others and tried not to ask for anything that wasn't vital.

Fezeka asked, "Zethu, don't you need new clothes?"

"Oh, I don't have money," Zethu answered.

"Did you ever have money before?" asked Fezeka.

"No."

"So when you need something, what do you usually do?"

Zethu laughed a little and said, "I ask you. But this isn't a priority. When you don't have money, you don't do these things."

"No, ma'am," responded Fezeka. "That's nonsense. You only graduate once, and you have to look like a graduate—any parent is going to make sure their child looks right."

<center>~~~~~~~</center>

Early one afternoon, I was in my office in the Ubuntu Centre, where I was entertaining a donor. He'd come down to visit—basically, to kick the tires of our operation and see where his money was going. Lots of donors have this impulse: They want to feel and see and hear what exactly their thousands of dollars have built. On this visit, I'd shown him around our multimillion-dollar, award-winning new home, which provided much-needed space for our after-school programs, tutoring, clinic, and pharmacy. We'd thrown a *braai*—a South African barbecue— in his honor, where he'd been able to meet many of our staff and students. Over a plate of roasted pig, he had heard about university plans, summer internships, and new jobs.

The donor's generosity didn't blind him to weaknesses in any organization, and he asked lots of probing, perceptive questions, gauging the return on his investment. Were we cost-effective? What impact did one of his dollars actually have? How were we reducing unnecessary costs? We'd been reviewing the details of Ubuntu's financial health for nearly an hour when a conversation outside my open door caught our attention.

"Zethu is graduating in a few days, and we want to buy her a new dress along with the graduation gown, and to take her to get her hair done," Fezeka was saying. "This is a big milestone. I think we should make her feel special."

"I don't know," we heard Jana, our program director, reply. "I'd love to do it for her, but does it make sense to spend the money there?"

"It's such a huge day for her, we have to celebrate," Fezeka responded. "You're right, of course," Jana said. "Let's look into it."

As they walked away, the donor looked at me with his eyebrows raised. "You can't possibly be considering buying one child new clothes for graduation, can you?" he said. "With all the strains on your budget, how could you possibly justify something so frivolous for a single girl?"

It was a fair question. What Ubuntu does—intensive, cradle-to-career services—costs a lot. In Zethu's case, her decade in our programs cost close to $65,000. In the world of development funding, where today's buzzwords are "scale," "sustainability," and "cost-effectiveness," this is a shocking number. Adding to that number by buying a special dress for a single occasion? Unthinkable.

But clearly Ubuntu doesn't follow the well-trod path. Later that afternoon, I talked to Fezeka, Jana, and other team members about giving Zethu a new dress. The unconditional feeling was "Of course we should do it! This is exactly *what* we do."

I thought again about Ubuntu's mission. It's more than metrics of cost and benefit, of return on investment—that's only one part of it. What we do, pure and simple, is help raise children. And part of raising children involves fielding those unexpected requests for things that may not be *necessary,* but make a child feel special.*

So, yeah, let's get Zethu that new dress. Let's make her feel amazing on this incredible day when she will become the first person, not only in her family but also on her entire street, to graduate from university.

---

* To be clear, Ubuntu also provides a high return on investment: Every dollar that Ubuntu Education Fund invests in a child results in real lifetime earnings of $8.70 and a $2.20 net gain to society.

Let's celebrate this accomplishment with her. Let's feel proud, like any parent would feel proud, and let's help her feel proud, too.

~~~~~~~

On graduation day, Fezeka went to pick up Zethu for the ceremony. She hadn't been able to go dress shopping with Zethu; Zethu had teased, "Good! You'd make me buy an old-lady dress." When Fezeka arrived, Zethu was putting on her final touches. After a few minutes, she emerged with a radiant smile, wearing a gray-and-navy dress that fell to just above her knees.

For a moment, Fezeka was silent. Then she said, "Wow—is that you? How come you are wearing this short dress?" She laughed, delighted at Zethu's transformation.

Zethu laughed, too, and said, "Ah, that is why I didn't want you to go shopping with me! This is what is being worn, and it's going to be under the gown anyway."

As she crossed the stage to collect her diploma a few hours later, Zethu paused to look out at the audience. Her sister, Lungi, was there, and her neighbors in the township, who had done all they could to watch out for her over the years. Fezeka was there, with tears in her eyes, and so was one of her teachers from high school, who had always treated her like a daughter.

After all that she'd been through, all the days of being overwhelmed and angry and sad, Zethu thought, this moment felt like the start of a new life. A pretty dress didn't make her a success, but it reminded her she'd become one.

CHAPTER TWO

A White Boy Walks into a *Shebeen*

THE *SHEBEEN* DIDN'T LOOK PARTICULARLY PROMISING. THE SUN WAS SET-ting in the New Brighton township of Port Elizabeth, and it was cold and drizzly. If I hadn't been twenty-one and up for adventure, I might have turned around. *Shebeens*—township bars that were illegal under apartheid—tended to be slapped-together affairs in someone's garage or apartment, a few benches and tables pulled together. This one badly needed a new coat of paint, and its corrugated tin roof looked like a stiff wind would send it flying. Still, it was full, with a crowd of middle-aged black South African men who crammed onto dark red, plastic-covered pleather benches. When I walked in, it was like a scene out of a movie: the needle scratching off the record, everyone turning to stare.

I'd met the guy who brought me there on a train earlier in the evening, when I'd had no idea where I was going. I'd landed in Cape Town the day before, after my advisor at the University of Pennsylvania, Dr. Mary Frances Berry, agreed to help me get credit for living and working in South Africa for four months during the summer of 1998.

I got to Cape Town at four in the afternoon, and by the next morning, I knew I couldn't stay. South Africa, after decades of apartheid and international isolation, offered a ripe target for predatory investors looking to take advantage of a fairly innocent business environment. The organization I had signed up with focused on environmental conservation. It was run by two guys who brought in international college students eager to volunteer, labor that appeared to benefit the founders more than any community.

I boarded the first train leaving Cape Town that night. It was one of those trains that stops *everywhere*: A trip that would take eight hours by car turned into a twenty-two-hour odyssey. So I had some time to talk with the guy sharing my compartment. He convinced me that I had to get off at Port Elizabeth, telling me, "It's sort of like your Detroit." It might be the first time that sales pitch worked.

If I had been more cautious, I probably wouldn't have agreed to go into New Brighton. The townships were notoriously dangerous; if you believed the newspapers, you'd expect to encounter a knife-wielding gangster on every corner. Add the fact that, as a white guy, I was a symbol of everything that was wrong with the country, and you get a situation that anyone in his right mind would want to avoid. But my new friend didn't seem worried as we stood in the doorway of that *shebeen*, so neither was I. Unfazed by the stares, he walked me in, sat me down at a table next to a rotund, cheerful-looking guy, said a few quick words in Xhosa, and left the two of us there. I found out later that he passed me off with the instruction, "I'm tired of speaking English. Why don't you talk to the kid?"

My new acquaintance gave me a warm smile and introduced himself as Banks. He put his arm around me and asked if I liked beer. These weren't your typical 12-ounce American beers; they were served in 36-ounce bottles and doled out into tiny water glasses. Over the next few hours, we split a dozen of them. He told me his nickname came from the great English goalkeeper Gordon Banks—"Because I was the best keeper in Port Elizabeth." I'd been a keeper, too, I told him. At the time, I was prouder of my accomplishments on the pitch than anything else I'd done, and that we had this in common seemed like a sign. Goalkeepers have to be a little crazy. It's all about taking chances, and following your impulse. Indecision is your worst enemy. You're by yourself while everybody else is out running around, and then, in an instant, you're diving headfirst at someone's feet.

Banks was a schoolteacher, and we quickly discovered that we had more in common than football. We both felt passionately about improving education and wanted to work within a community to make a difference. Several hours later, we were ready to leave, and I explained my predicament: I couldn't stay at that nonprofit in Cape Town. But I couldn't let Professor Berry down, either. I didn't want to know what she would do to me if I did. I needed to come up with a new project, and I wanted to be somewhere where my presence had a positive effect. Banks offered, "Come work in my school. It's as poor a school as any."

"That's great, Banks," I said. "But where am I going to live?"

"You'll live with me," he responded, flashing that huge grin.

~~~~~~

I was born in New York City, but by the time I was a toddler, my parents had moved us out to New Jersey. South Orange was a leafy suburb about a half hour outside Manhattan, but it felt thousands of miles away; it was the kind of sleepy, comfortable place where no one left and no one new arrived. My father worked at Goldman Sachs, and my mother built and ran the library at a school for autistic children.

Our next-door neighbors were my Aunt Dottie and Uncle Tom, who gave me my first taste of entrepreneurship. They ran a highly success-ful washer-and-dryer business in East Orange that they had built from scratch. I'd go out to their warehouse and marvel at the huge space filled with machines. It seemed very glamorous to me: to work for yourself, to create something out of nothing. It may not have been Mark Zuckerberg starting Facebook out of his dorm room, but it had a huge impact on me.

When I was fourteen, we moved to London. The city itself was a revelation, but the most remarkable, transformative aspect was my high school, the American School in London. Social consciousness was the norm, probably an effect of the school's cosmopolitanism. Fifty-seven nations were represented in the student body. Within weeks of my enrollment, a class field trip took us to Prague, and my football team went to tournaments in Vienna and Budapest. One of the first major events after I arrived was "Middle East night" to raise money for Pales-tinian refugees—certainly not what a Jewish kid from New Jersey was used to. My friends came from all over the world: Kuwait, Colombia, Iran, Greece.

I'd long had an interest in South Africa. I'd never been there, but one of my first memories is of seeing the iconic Keith Haring *Free South Africa* poster in the window of a frame shop in New Jersey. In school, I'd read books like *Kaffir Boy,* Mark Mathabane's visceral recollection of growing up in the townships, and in London, exiled activists had turned the city into a center of the antiapartheid move-ment, frequently protesting in front of South Africa House in Tra-falgar Square. So in 1992, after watching Nelson Mandela be freed from prison and the dismantling of apartheid rapidly accelerating, I approached a teacher, John Otterpohl, at my school about taking a trip to South Africa.

This wasn't out of the blue: Mr. Otterpohl ran a program called Study Tours: Cultural Immersion that let students study an area of con-flict and then arrange a trip to that area. One year, a group of students visited Israel and Palestine and met with Yasir Arafat; another year the destination was Cuba and a meeting with Fidel Castro. Mr. Otterpohl agreed to my idea for a trip, and then he turned over the task of figuring out all the logistics to my classmates and me.

After nearly eighteen months of preparation, we landed in Johannesburg in May of 1994 for six weeks of exploration. Our group—fifteen high school students representing twelve nationalities, and three chaperones—crowded into a *combi,* a small van, to make our way into the city. Euphoria filled the air. Racial tension and segregation have plagued South Africa since the first European settlers arrived in the seventeenth century, but the systematic program of discrimination and oppression known as apartheid was put in place in 1948, when the National Party, under the leadership of Daniel François Malan, rose to power on a platform of racial segregation. Under the party's government, a series of restrictive laws were passed: the Prohibition of Mixed Marriages Act and the Immorality Amendment Act, which forbade interracial unions; the Population Registration Act, which classified all citizens by race using a set of arbitrary racial characteristics; and the Group Areas Act, which established separate urban areas delineated by race.

Black residents were required to carry passbooks bearing photographs and fingerprints wherever they went, and the everyday elements of life—getting a job, riding the bus, finding a place to live—were burdened with layers of bureaucracy. Under apartheid, black workers were pressed into de facto slavery: often separated from their families, their movements restricted, their wages a fraction of those of white workers. The African National Congress (ANC) had been established in 1912, but its mission sharpened in the face of a government regime of racism. Leaders like Walter Sisulu, Nelson Mandela, Oliver Tambo, and Govan Mbeki (the father of Thabo Mbeki, who became president of South Africa following Mandela) advocated nonviolent protest and then, in the face of intractable racial hatred, armed resistance. In 1990, after years of struggle, years of violence and terror, years of the police torturing suspects in jails, of resisters turning on potential informers,

of destabilization and international isolation, the National Party government, under F. W. de Klerk, finally conceded defeat and began to
turn the country into a true democracy.

It's almost impossible to convey the strength of the emotions at
play in South Africa in those years. People embraced their New South
Africa, acting like proud parents of a child done well. In his inaugural
address, Nelson Mandela acknowledged the feeling of triumph while
pressing the need for forgiveness, saying, "The time for the healing of
the wounds has come. The moment to bridge the chasms that divide us
has come. The time to build is upon us." Yet underneath these feelings
of victorious joy remained an edge of anger and pain. My classmates
and I were a bunch of teenagers ill-equipped to understand these complicated emotions, but we thought of ourselves as diplomats. We'd studied everything there was to study on South Africa, talked to everyone
we could in London, and we figured we knew all there was to know.
Turns out, we were better prepared for a Model United Nations conference than postapartheid South Africa.

The highlight of the trip was supposed to be spending time with
Nelson Mandela, with whom we had arranged to meet one week in July.
As the date approached, though, his office called to cancel: He had to
have emergency cataract surgery. During his imprisonment on Robben
Island, he'd been conscripted into breaking limestone for days on end;
the searing glare off the white rock had badly damaged his eyes. Mandela's office arranged for us to meet instead with Walter Sisulu, the former president of the ANC who had been jailed with Mandela. We had
tea with him at the ANC headquarters on Bree Street. Mr. Sisulu might
have been the most dignified man I've ever met, and his gray hair and
kind eyes made him seem the wisest. At the same time, you could sense
that Mr. Sisulu lacked some of the indomitable will that distinguished
Mandela as the father of his nation and made him such a powerful chief.
Ahmed Kathrada, an ANC member and fellow prisoner, once said of
Mandela and Sisulu, "Mandela was highly respected, highly admired.

But I would not be able to say he was as loved as Sisulu was. You know that difference between a father and a leader? That was the big difference between them."

We spent hours in conversation with anyone we could persuade to meet with us: CEOs, political leaders, fish-and-chip shop owners, homeless people. We met with members of the Afrikaner Weerstandsbeweging (AWB), the far-right-wing party, who reluctantly agreed to host our many students of color, but refused to take questions from them. We talked to many victims of apartheid, who were unsparing in their descriptions of brutality: constant raids by the police, unremitting poverty, rape, and torture. These conversations had the same honesty, the same desire to bare the wounds of the past fifty years, that later characterized the Truth and Reconciliation hearings, the groundbreaking airing of terrorization, torture, and murder that had been committed under apartheid. The pain they related was searing and raw: This had happened to their uncles, their brothers, themselves.

What made it more challenging was that it was difficult to look at South Africa and say, unequivocally, here are the good guys and here are the bad guys. You had the Inkatha Freedom Party, a largely Zulu organization that was being armed by the AWB and slaughtering Xhosa communities in the run-up to the elections.* There were intense power struggles over who would lead the next government. And, of course, there was the tension between the freedom fighters and activists, who had stayed in the country and felt as though they had earned the right to lead but had been denied an education that would help them do so, and the exiles returning to the country, who had the intellectual and

---

* The black population of South Africa consists of a number of tribes, including Zulu and Xhosa, among many others. (This diversity is reflected in South Africa's eleven official languages.) While there was a factional split between the Zulu and the Xhosas during apartheid—the former largely associated with the Inkatha Freedom Party, and the latter with the ANC—the antiapartheid movement always maintained a high degree of inclusivity. In the postapartheid era, members of the ANC leadership represent every faction of South African society.

educational experience but had been absent from the realities of South Africa some for decades.

A chaperone on our trip, Tommy Maxoli, was one of those exiles. We'd met him as we began studying the country, and, while he wasn't a teacher at my school, he became an integral part of our group. He'd left South Africa twenty years earlier for London, and this was the first time he'd returned. The idea of going into exile has always hit me hard: leaving your home at a moment's notice in the middle of the night, abandoning all your possessions, not saying good-bye to your family. This was Tommy's story. I'd never met anyone who loved and pined for his home as much as he did.

One night, he decided to take us out to Long Street, the Bourbon Street of Cape Town. The area had always been whites only, but, Tommy figured, anyone was allowed to go anywhere in South Africa now. Tommy was so excited to take our group—a racially mixed bunch of foreigners—out to party. We were happy to relieve the tension of these long days with some beers. We'd all had several—Tommy probably more than anyone—when a white guy started harassing Tommy. The guy yelled out, "Hey *kaffir*,* get out of here! No *kaffir*s allowed!"

Tommy, maybe emboldened by the alcohol but also by the feeling that his country was his again, squared up to him and said, "I have every right to be here." And with one punch the guy knocked him out.

The punch shattered Tommy. More than the physical pain, he was embarrassed, he was hurt, and he felt let down. He had imagined his return so often over the years, and had yearned for it desperately. To him, London was just a place, his real life in abeyance. South Africa was his home and his refuge, and once apartheid was over, he'd be able to return and live there the way he was always meant to. But he would never be the same after that punch, that reminder that things hadn't changed, at least not nearly enough. He was a man of no country, with nowhere to call home.

---

* A racial slur..

~~~~~~

As we traveled around the country, the tension throughout South Africa began to take a toll on our little group—we all had trouble dealing with the intensity of it. We began arguing, verbal sniping that escalated finally into a physical fight between two of my classmates. The trip was supposed to be about absorbing everything—but we didn't actually make sense of anything. And Mr. Otterpohl didn't have the nurturing spirit that might have helped ease the way for some of us. For him, it was *Tuck your shirt in, bury your emotions, and toughen up.*

But Mr. Otterpohl did know how to challenge us intellectually, and how to get us to interact with ordinary people. He'd accompany us to formal meetings, whether it was with a CEO or a government minister, and then he'd suddenly say, "Okay, let's get out of here." He'd pick the craziest places for us to go, push us out of that little *combi,* and tell us, "Walk around." He'd told all of us to bring a thousand balloons, without telling us why. Once we got there, he directed, "Go make friends with the kids—blow up balloons with them, give them some stickers. Then everyone else will love you." And you know what? It worked.

One of these jaunts landed us in Alexandra township, in the shadow of Sandton, the wealthiest suburb on the continent. Sandton is known as Africa's richest square mile; it houses both the places to make money—financial firms, the stock exchange—and the places to spend it—designer shops like Gucci, Cartier, and Louis Vuitton. Alexandra township, crowded with tin shacks and muddy roads, houses the domestic workers who support Sandton. As usual, Mr. Otterpohl had shoved us out of the van to walk around, explore, and talk to as many people as we could. The sun was starting to set, and the shadows of Sandton's skyscrapers crept over the township. A group of barefoot children was playing a game in the street, running and laughing. A *gogo** was standing next to me, watching the kids, too, and we started

---

* An affectionate Xhosa term for "granny."

talking. She was a large woman, wearing a flower-patterned dress, and her huge smile offset her imposing dignity. When I told her that we were here to learn about the New South Africa, she told me about waiting in line for five days to cast her ballot "for Madiba"—the first time I'd heard anyone refer to Mandela by his clan name. I thought to myself, *This woman could barely stand for an hour, much less wait in line for five days.* So I said, maybe a little skeptically, "You waited five days to vote?"

She chuckled and patted me on the shoulder. "No, boy," she told me. "I waited for eighty-five years."

I'd grown up in a privileged home, I'd always gone to nice schools, and I'd never had to ask myself what freedom meant. Here, in this New South Africa, people were full of hope and fervently believed that they could make their lives better. I looked around, at the kids in the township playing happily among the shacks, at this woman who had waited her entire life to take part in the most fundamental rite of citizenship, and I thought to myself, *This is for me. I want to be part of this.*

~~~~~~

About this time, I'd started to think about university. I wanted to go somewhere that would match the civic engagement and diversity of my high school experience. When I arrived at Penn in the fall of 1995, my first feeling was disappointment. I assumed that this stellar university, one of the best in the country, which drew students from all over the world, would be cosmopolitan and inclusive. In reality, I'd never been anywhere so segregated. Everyone sorted themselves into dorms based on race, religion, or ethnicity. I thought there would be a lottery system randomly assigning us to room with new people. Instead, we were allowed to retreat into the groups that made us the most comfortable. Coming from a high school where classmates from nearly sixty countries mixed freely, the self-constrained social groups felt claustrophobic.

The summer after my freshman year at Penn, I went to Maine,

where my parents then lived and ran a restaurant, and worked with them. I decided, *I'm not going back, I'm going to stay here.* For the next year, I worked on a lobster boat, *Just A Pluggin'.* I spent my days baiting bags and cutting fish for hours on end. It was physically exhausting and repetitive, but it cleared my mind; I'd be doing the same tasks—pulling out and slicing open maggot-filled herrings to lure in the lobsters, cleaning out the lobster traps and throwing back all the other sea creatures we'd inadvertently caught—and the whole time, I'd be thinking and planning. At the end of the year, I realized, *Hey, if I want to get back to South Africa, I need to get my degree and prepare myself.* I went back to Penn with a different attitude.

That fall, I threw myself into finding courses that honestly meant something to me. I was a history student, but I didn't want to sit in a classroom and talk about who did what in World War II. I wanted to talk about issues that affect people in the here and now, and I wanted professors who would force us students to broach uncomfortable subjects and interrogate our beliefs. I started taking a class with Dr. Peter Conn, who came up with a program called Academically Based Community Service, which alternated time in the classroom with practical experience in the field, spending time in communities affected by issues we'd studied. Dr. Conn pressed us to have frank discussions about politics and history, and how those subjects might affect the people we interact with on a daily basis. We had to consider our own assumptions, tear them down, and build up a new way of thinking.

I also sought out another professor, Dr. Mary Frances Berry. She was formidable, having served in President Jimmy Carter's cabinet and as chancellor of the University of Colorado Boulder. She was the only person to successfully sue a president, after Ronald Reagan dismissed her from the US Commission on Civil Rights; she was reinstated and served until 2004. Dr. Berry also helped found the Free South Africa movement, and had been arrested many times for her activism in the cause. Her classes were full, but I bugged her until she let me in one.

Six of us sat around her office, which was filled with photos of Dr. Berry with Jesse Jackson and Dr. Berry with Nelson Mandela, and discussed law and policy. Dr. Berry exuded vitality. Unlike some professors who analyze but never engage with the world, she exerted her intellectual rigor on real problems, and took action. She was intimidating, no doubt, but she also listened carefully to her students, and supported them.

Following the activist examples of Dr. Berry and Dr. Conn, I started working at the university's Center for Community Partnerships. It was well intentioned—we volunteered in disadvantaged schools and community projects in West Philadelphia, much of which was impoverished. I'm sure that there were those who found our presence helpful, and I loved working with the kids. But from this experience, I learned mostly about how not to engage in development. The program was infected with an us-and-them mentality, on both sides. Since then, the center's approach has evolved, and by all reports its programs have dramatically improved. But at the time, it felt like a bunch of privileged university students, full of bravado, providing what were ultimately rather shallow services.

If anything, it made me more eager to get back to South Africa to try to figure out what I could do there. I persuaded Dr. Berry to act as an advisor and help me get credit for a self-created study-abroad program over the summer. I, along with my friends Dan Byrd and Dan Friedland, signed up to volunteer with an environmental group, and my plan was to keep journals of my work for Dr. Berry. I was so eager to get to South Africa that I arranged to take my final exams early and flew out before the semester ended.

For someone interested in development, South Africa offered tons of opportunity. Post-1994, the country had been flooded with new organizations eager to be a part of the opening society—but many of them, including nonprofits, exploited the situation for their own gain. When I got to Cape Town and showed up at the group's office, I saw a bunch of young international students helping to generate money for no discernible purpose other than to line the founders' pockets. I thought, *Are you out of your minds?*

So there I was in the *shebeen.*

And, with hardly a second thought, I'd decided to spend the next three months in a South African township defined by intense poverty and crippling violence, where my white skin symbolized oppression, with a guy I'd just met over a beer.

CHAPTER THREE

One Crazy Summer in the Townships

WE MADE OUR WAY FROM THE *SHEBEEN* TO BANKS'S PLACE. HE LIVED IN what were known as the railway flats—originally built for railway workers, they were a step up from the shacks, but still shabby, small, and poorly constructed. The staircases were dark and narrow, filled with an overpowering scent of urine. Broken glass littered the hallways, and the pulsating beat of *kwaito*, a kind of house music particular to the townships, provided background noise all day and all night.

None of this bothered me too much. I was drunk, I was a kid, I had my backpack with all of my possessions, and I was going to have a roof over my head. We went up to the second story and opened the door to Banks's flat. It hadn't crossed my mind before, but of course Banks didn't live alone. His girlfriend, Mickey, and his son, Mlingani, and his daughter, Nomatola, who were just a year or two younger than me, were all home when we got there, and they were terrified at the sight of me. They assumed I was the police.

I had no idea what was going on, but I could tell that Mickey was giving Banks an earful. I'd say it roughly translated to "Are you out of your mind, bringing this white guy home?" It hadn't occurred to Banks that maybe he should run this idea past the people he was living with. His impulse was "Hold on, this is a young guy who's alone in a foreign land, and it's my job to take him in." He told Mickey, "Oh, he's okay. I've been drinking beers with him." After what felt like an hour of angry scolding, Banks prevailed; he told me to put my bag on his son's mattress, because I'd be sleeping there with Mlingani.

"You must be hungry," Banks said and opened up the fridge. "I've got some real bachelor food here." He pulled out a sheep's head, threw a handful of salt on it, and set it down in front of me. "Let's eat!" he commanded. I didn't even know where to begin. Banks went straight for the eyeball, plucked it out, and tossed it in his mouth.

The next day, he took me to his school, Emfundweni Primary School. Along with most of the schools in the township, it had been established under the Bantu Education Act,* the brainchild of Hendrik Verwoerd. As minister of native affairs, and later as prime minister, Verwoerd decided that there was no reason to offer true education and opportunity to a class of people who should aspire to be only manual laborers. He wrote, "What is the use of teaching a Bantu child mathematics when it cannot use it in practice?" The buildings themselves spoke to this philosophy: They were big brick bunkers, meant to impede learning and stifle motivation. The antiapartheid movement in large

---

* Originally referring to Bantu-speaking peoples of sub-Saharan Africa, the term "Bantu," one of four official racial categories, was adopted in South Africa to refer to black Africans. The segregated homelands that the National Party created in order to deny black residents South African citizenship were originally referred to as Bantustans.

measure grew out of this oppression. Many of the most significant protests revolved around the issue of equal education—for the parents, aunts and uncles, and grandparents, who were largely illiterate, what mattered was to ensure that their children had the opportunity to go to school. And the students felt the weight of this responsibility.

At Emfundweni, there were easily sixty children in every class, crammed three or four to a desk. The tight space meant that they all wrote in a crabbed, tiny script, which still managed to be entirely legible—much better than my handwriting. The kids remained totally silent at all times; the teacher could leave the room for an hour and there wouldn't be a peep. What's more, there were often no walls separating the classes: in one room, fifty or sixty students would sit facing the east wall, another fifty or sixty facing the west, sitting back-to-back where the classes met in the middle. At the time, Banks taught two classes, a seventh-grade science class and a sixth-grade math class. He'd stand on one side of the classroom, lead the sixth graders through a math problem, and then run to the other side of the room to teach the seventh graders about photosynthesis. He ran back and forth, one side to the next, all day, the only teacher for more than a hundred students.

Banks showed me around the school. Most of the classrooms had broken windows, and all the floors were mud. During breaks in the day, the girls would go out and get buckets of water to clean and smooth the floors. (The boys would go out in the field and play.) Yet in the courtyard of this dilapidated, fetid building grew a lush, gorgeous garden. Banks had decided that the children deserved a beautiful place amid the squalor; he couldn't renovate the building itself, so he created what he called his botanical gardens, a little oasis of indigenous greenery.

Finally, we went to meet the principal, Mr. Nondikane, who I'd heard had been a great teacher earlier in his career but was now weighed down by the enormity of his job. We talked for a while about what I could do. I suggested an after-school program to be based on work I'd done with kids in West Philadelphia. I'd spend time mentoring high school students, and they in turn would mentor primary school students. The principal liked the sound of it, but told me I'd need to persuade the school governing body, a group of parents and teachers who help run the school. I spent a couple of days talking to the members, telling them about my experiences working elsewhere. I did the same at Ndzondelelo, the neighboring high school. At last, everyone agreed to let me set up a small program, which I called A Study in Self-Reliance.

My first day, I walked into the classroom and found eight high school students waiting for me. It hit me: I was only three or four years older than they were. How was I supposed to be an authority figure? But I plunged ahead and asked the group what they wanted to accomplish. The first one to speak was Mzi. He wore meticulously pressed trousers, a tie, and a sports jacket—and even though his clothes were probably two sizes too big for him, he carried himself with enormous dignity. He asked if we could do some experiments, "because I'd like to become a scientist." Everyone else agreed—they hardly ever got the chance to do hands-on work in the classroom. I'm a disaster at science, and I wasn't exactly qualified to be designing experiments, but I thought, *I can put something together*. That night, I asked Banks, naively, "Where's the supply room at school?"

He gave me a look and said, "What do you mean?"

"You know, the kids want to do some science experiments, so I thought I'd get some supplies."

Banks shook his head. "Why don't you take them for a walk and see what you find?"

So the next day the eight students and I left the classroom to scavenge materials for a science experiment. We made our way to a neighboring dump and picked up some old batteries and wires. Back in the classroom, Mzi led the effort, disconnecting and reconnecting the wires until he found the right combination. Another student had picked up a propeller, and they improvised a hookup to the battery. The propeller started to turn—slowly at first, but gradually picking up momentum, until it was whirling at top speed. Mzi was too reserved to let out a whoop, but he smiled shyly and proudly and said, "We did it, didn't we?"

~~~~~~~

That summer, since I didn't go to the school until later in the afternoon, my mornings were spent exploring the townships and meeting as many people as I could. I'd either walk or flag down a *combi,* the primary form of public transportation in the area. They looked like minivans, but the floor was often rusted through in spots, and they'd be crammed with what felt like dozens of adults and crying babies and overflowing bags of groceries, all held together by string, duct tape, and prayer. I'm not a religious person, but every time I got on one of those, I thought, *God, please let me make it off this thing.* No matter where I went, people were warm and friendly, and everyone seemed happy to talk with me. As the first white person to live in this area, I was a novelty, even a bit of a celebrity. The kids would come up and rub my legs, amazed by how hairy they were. It was a stereotypical white-man-in-Africa experience.

I asked a lot of questions those mornings, and I heard lots of powerful, heartbreaking stories. Emotions were still raw from the years of apartheid. The Eastern Cape in general, and Port Elizabeth in particular, incubated many of the leaders of the antiapartheid movement. Steve Biko, the founder of the Black Consciousness Movement, was born in the Eastern Cape. In 1977, he was taken into custody in Port Elizabeth, when he received the injuries that would cause his death, making him one of the most infamous victims of police brutality. His sister lived down the street from Banks and me. Chris Hani, who had been the chief of staff of the African National Congress (ANC) armed resistance wing and was assassinated in 1993, grew up in the Transkei, and his name is still graffitied across walls in the township neighborhoods. Mandela himself grew up in the Eastern Cape. The Transkei was the first of the "separate areas," or Bantustans, which were a key element of the apartheid system: homelands for black South Africans that would operate independently of white South Africa, which typically meant having no access to natural resources, prime agricultural land, or any means of economic development. The old government used to think that if they could keep the Eastern Cape subdued, they could maintain apartheid. So they strangled the region.

Of course, I knew the history. I'd studied the Rivonia Trial, which resulted in the long imprisonment of Mandela, Sisulu, and six of their comrades; the 1960 Sharpeville massacre, in which sixty-nine people protesting the repressive passbook laws were shot and killed by police; and the Soweto uprising, which began on June 16, 1976, in response to a new edict requiring schools to teach in Afrikaans, and which resulted in hundreds of dead and wounded students. But the stories I heard that summer were just as terrible, just as troubling, and they had happened to the people who lived next door to me. Everyone I met had a story: Anele, in flat 21, had been jailed as a sixteen-year-old and gone on a forty-two-day hunger strike. Lungi, the tavern queen who ran our local *shebeen,* had a father who was politically active; when she was thirteen, the police raided their home in the middle of the night, raped her, and stuck a gun in her father's mouth. Everyone constantly felt tension, fear, and confusion. Why was this happening to them? Why were they being persecuted for simply living their lives? When apartheid finally crumbled, people were filled with hope. No one would harass them for walking down the wrong street; no one would force their way into their homes. But all of the entrenched problems remained: poverty, crime, bad schools, and no jobs. It was 1998, and the township was still a township.

Often I heard people ask, How has my life changed? "It was better during apartheid, because at least I had" this or that. Unemployment had increased, and while the ANC had promised huge improvements—improved education, increased access to utilities, better housing—they came slowly. How could the ANC do it all? They inherited a bankrupt government, a society that had been deeply fractured, and terrible infrastructure problems.

I'd never experienced this kind of poverty before. It was everywhere. Nobody had enough food to eat. Nobody was working. When you had tea at someone's house, they would take their tea bag, put it on the wall to dry, and then use it again later. I was hypersensitive about spending any money; I wanted to be a part of the community, for all its good and all its ills. So, like everyone else, I didn't eat a whole lot. Our daily meals were bread, potatoes, and, if we were lucky, some gravy with bits of meat. When the money started to run out at the end of the month, we'd resort to what I'd call bowl o' starch: noodles, torn-up pieces of bread, and mashed potatoes, mixed up with a bunch of mayonnaise. (It didn't taste like much, but it filled us up.) And many days, we survived on beer and Simba chips.*

Despite the challenges, there was an overwhelming sense of pride in the country, a determination to turn those years of fighting for freedom into positive growth. I never felt like South Africa was on the brink of failure. Opportunities to move into the black middle class did expand. Yet I could see that too many were still left behind.

~~~~~~~

All this time, my friendship with Banks was growing deeper. He is a complicated man, and in many ways, like me, he didn't always conform to the rules of society. But he has enormous energy and love for his community, and he wants to devote everything he can to it. He would take kids off the streets and give them a place to sleep, and constantly ran programs at the school after other teachers went home. He led an effort to beautify the campus—the origin of the courtyard garden—because he understood that improving your surroundings can help make striving for something better feel a little more possible. In a different place and time, he would have gone to graduate school and

---

* The ubiquitous snack of South Africa, with a little smiling lion mascot on every package.

earned a master's degree in education. But he grew up under apartheid, when a black man's choices were basically to become a farm laborer, a mine worker, or a garden boy. If you happened to catch someone's eye, you might get to go to Teacher's College, though even that was nothing more than a glorified high school. This is where Banks had ended up. And yet within these straitened circumstances, Banks found a way to enlarge his life and those of the people around him.

Of course, I wasn't living only with Banks: I was living with Banks's son and his girlfriend, Mickey, too. (Nomatola lived at her university.) Harmony did not always reign. One day, Banks and Mickey had a terrible argument that resulted in their splitting up. Mickey packed a bag and left. That evening, Banks and I had cooked dinner and were eating in the living room, watching a football game on television. Suddenly, a loud knocking interrupted us.

Banks got up to answer the door and Mickey stormed in, clearly angry. "I want my plates," she announced—the ones our dinner was rapidly cooling on.

Banks looked at me sheepishly and said, "Jake, I think you should leave for a bit."

I went a couple doors down to the local *shebeen* to wait for him. A few hours later, Banks showed up. "I'm sorry about this," he mumbled. "I didn't think she'd be so upset."

When we got back to the apartment, it was totally bare. There was no furniture, no TV, just two teacups in an otherwise bare cupboard. And it stayed that way for the rest of my time there.

~~~~~~

Banks's apartment building faced a big empty lot. It didn't look very promising—the ground was hard-packed dirt, strewn with glass— but every day a football team took the field to practice. I'd been a keeper for many years, and I was still obsessed with the sport. I thought maybe I could play with the team, get out and kick the ball around a bit. I asked for the coach, and someone pointed out a guy in a little gray fisherman's cap. I walked over and introduced myself. He told me his name was Rasta Chris and invited me to sit down and watch the team practice. The players trained to a beat—they would chant as they passed the ball or practiced their footwork. It was incredibly rhythmic, and far different from any practice I'd ever taken part in. It took a lot of work to maintain once I started practicing with them.

But on this day I was only observing, and when drills were over, Chris invited me over to his flat. It was nuts. Chris had painted his place bright green, with yellow splotches everywhere: Rastafarian Central. He asked me, "Do you smoke?" and pulled out a huge brown envelope of South African weed, or *dagga,* which was cheap and plentiful in the townships. He rolled a *zol** as big as my forearm, and handed it to me. Then he started rolling another one, and I realized that the first huge *zol* was just for me. We sat back, smoking and drifting through conversation as we listened to Bob Marley on a 1980s boom box.

As much as I enjoyed getting out and playing football, I was out of shape and could barely keep up with the younger guys, so being on the team was really about hanging out with Chris. We became very close. Chris was Sotho, fairly uncommon for our area, which was almost solely Xhosa, and he worked in a supermarket as a shelver. He loved the boys on his team, and he would always have them over to his flat and buy them soda and a loaf of bread if he had the money. He had this great old 1970s BMW painted six shades of brown; big black and gold banners for his favorite team, the Kaiser Chiefs, covered the back windows. He'd draped the seats with animal skins from the ritual slaughtering they'd do whenever he went back to his village—his mother was a *sangoma,* a cross between a traditional healer and a witch doctor.

What I most liked about Chris was that, like me, he didn't entirely belong there. Chris had lived in a lot of different places and had done

---

* South African slang for a joint.

lots of different things. He was a worldly guy, in the best sense of the word, even though he'd never lived overseas. He was open to new experiences in a way that many people from the townships didn't know how to be. It's so easy to be blinkered to the world around you when you are from a place like that, when it's so difficult to get out and when every day is about survival. In many ways, Chris showed me how important it is to be able to imagine life outside of the townships. Later, I realized that an inability to do this, through inexperience or disinterest, often constitutes the biggest obstacle for people in the townships—if you can't imagine it, you can't dream of being a part of it.

Another good friend, Sloo, showed me the flip side of all this, how easy and seductive township life can be. Sloo was a wannabe *tsotsi*, a gangster, and when we hung out, it was guaranteed to be wild: girls, parties, and trouble. He played on Chris's team, and he dreamed about being a hairdresser. (A gangster football player who wants to style hair— you can't make this up.) But he wanted, more than anything, to smoke a whole phone book. No one had money for rolling papers, so he'd stolen a phone book from the city and would use its pages to roll giant *zols*. I helped him get through some of the As. But I had to be careful with Sloo. He and his gangster buddies weren't killing people, but their escapades weren't innocent, either. Sloo was the kind of guy who couldn't fathom a life outside the townships. He's lived—and probably will die—without ever seriously venturing out of them.

<hr />

Each afternoon, I'd show up at the school around 2:00 p.m. and join Mzi and the other high school students in one of the classrooms. Sometimes we'd discuss their schoolwork, but sometimes we'd simply talk about their dreams and their goals. I wanted to help raise the students' self-esteem, build their confidence, and teach them how to be role models. Just to have a sympathetic ear meant a great deal to them, and receiving any sort of personal attention seemed to have a transformative effect. In turn, we'd go over to the primary school and meet with a group of sixteen kids there. The older kids would tutor them, and I'd walk around to help and make the same efforts at building confidence and self-esteem.

One of my favorites of the younger students was Sindi, who, like many of her peers, had an extremely unstable home life. Her father was chronically unemployed and drank too much, her mother had died, and her stepmother was mentally ill, and there was very little money for food or other basic necessities. She was petite, with a head of golden red hair and big brown eyes, and she was incredibly bright and full of ambition. With Banks's encouragement, she had entered a science contest and won, and was supposed to go to Cape Town for the next stage of the competition. But she needed four hundred rand—about eighty bucks—to make the trip, and she didn't have it. I was at home when Banks came running in. "Sindi is in the hospital," he told me. "She tried to kill herself. She ate a bunch of pills."

Banks and I went straight to the hospital. I was clearly in over my head, and, for the first time, I doubted my own strength to work in the townships. It was heartbreaking; a twelve-year-old girl shouldn't try to kill herself. Navigating the hallways of the immense hospital, Dora Nginza, took forever. The cavernous, worn-down facility was crammed with sick and distraught people, without nearly enough beds for all of them. The beleaguered staff had no idea where anyone was, and only after we'd wandered around for half an hour, peering into rooms, did we find Sindi, who'd been placed on a small cot. She looked bruised and fragile and so small. Banks and I sat next to her, and I took her hand. "You have to come to us," I told her. "We're here for you. We'll always try to get you what you need, even if it feels like too much to ask."

I realized that, while the work I did helped, there was so much more to be done. Sindi excelled at school, but she'd go home to a terrible situation: a sick stepmother, little food, siblings who depended on her. Sindi needed not only emotional support and counseling but also for the people around her to be taken care of so they could take care of her. It was an important lesson that there's so much you can't control. You can't always know the pressures kids feel, or protect them from their parents or the violence of the townships, or even from themselves.

〰〰〰〰

Banks loved to issue orders. He'd tell me, "It's time to play pool" or "It's time to drink," and that's what we'd do. I was happy to have him instructing me. I thought of Banks as the mayor of the township. Everyone knew him, he knew everyone, and he seemed eager to play the role of my social director. One day, Banks came back to the flat and told me, "This man, Pumi,* he lives in number 56, he'd like to invite you to a culturework. His son is coming from the bush." This was circumcision, one of the major rituals of Xhosa life, when all the teenage boys retreat to the bush for six weeks. The first day, they line up and get snipped. Shedding even a single tear is not an option. Every day, the men of the tribe hike out to the bush and talk about what it's like to be a man, their new responsibilities, and the traditions of the tribe. Mandela described the ritual's solemnity by saying, "An uncircumcised Xhosa man is a contradiction in terms, for he is not considered a man at all, but a boy."†

Pumi had been in exile in Sweden in the 1980s before coming back to the townships, and his family's ancestral home was in the Karoo, the large semidesert area to the northwest of Port Elizabeth. My friends Dan Friedland and Dan Byrd, who were working elsewhere in South Africa, happened to be visiting at the time, so we all piled into Pumi's *baki*—a pickup truck with a cover over the back. It should have been a three-hour drive, but we kept stopping to pick up more and more peo-

---

* Pumi died recently, in his mid-forties. The most shocking thing about his death was how commonplace the news felt: So many of the men and women who have made up my South Africa experience have died at a young age.

† Mandela wrote a wonderful chapter on the ritual in his autobiography, *Long Walk to Freedom*.

ple, so it ended up taking closer to six. Someone took out a bottle of brandy and started passing it around.

Around eight that evening we finally arrived, and fourteen of us tumbled out into the hot, dusty Karoo night. The family was in the middle of preparations for the weekend. At any culturework, there's a lot of slaughtering, a lot of eating, a lot of drinking. They make huge vats of *umqomboti,* a traditional beer that tastes like a blue cheese–and-sawdust milk shake. That night, Pumi's family killed six sheep, and the family and their guests had the honor of eating the innards. Somehow, I got handed a penis. I didn't want to be rude, so I took a little bite. It was vile. I noticed that my friend Dan F. hadn't been paying attention, so I foisted it off on him by saying, "Oh, Pumi wanted you to have this. He insisted." By now everyone had turned around and was looking at him. Dan did the honorable thing and choked all of it down.

We spent the night on the floor of the family's little house, about thirty of us all crammed in together. The next day, we got up very early, and all the men hiked up to where the boys were and took them to a river. Once the boys are circumcised, they're painted white, so the ancestors won't recognize them in this ambiguous state, between boyishness and manhood. Each boy had what they call an uncle, basically a family mentor, and on this day, the uncles washed the white paint off the boys with butter. Then they painted the boys red, and gave them beautiful Lesotho blankets. All the boys had *indukus*—fighting sticks— and we marched the two kilometers back to the village together, singing, dancing, and stick fighting.

When we finally made it back to the village, the families held their own celebrations. Each boy retreated to a special room where people came in and made offerings to him—mostly a cent of a cent. By this point, it was about 8:30 in the morning, and drinking was already underway. The men and women sat separately, in huge circles called *kraals,* and passed around buckets of *umqomboti*—like a bad college drinking game. Meat began to circulate as well—chunks of sheep that had been boiled in a little bit of water and seasoned with the animal's blood.

The family had set aside the sheep's head, and we ate that the next day, before we got back into the *baki* to make the long drive to Port Elizabeth. Once again, a bottle of brandy came out, but this time I was in the front seat and realized that the driver was taking plenty of swigs, too. Between three of us, we finished the whole bottle.

That kind of drinking—heavy and reckless—was commonplace that summer. Every social event revolved around alcohol. As a twenty-one-year-old kid, I loved it. I was having the time of my life. Of course, I romanticized both the partying and the poverty. But I think my willingness to throw myself into these extreme social situations helped me become a part of the township life. If I'd been more cautious, more sober (in both senses of the word), I wouldn't have been able to open myself up to this kind of life. I probably wouldn't have been in the township at all, to be honest.

Most weekend nights, somebody would be throwing a party in their flat. It'd be a tiny room, packed with people, no ventilation, everyone dancing and sweating and drinking and smoking. No one bought packs of cigarettes—they were too expensive. We'd go to the *spaza* shop, basically a convenience store run out of someone's house, and buy one or two cigarettes and share them. You'd never see anyone smoking his own cigarette. These parties would go on for hours, with people passing around cheap brandy, joints, sometimes pills. I'd get tired, but no one else ever appeared to. And I'd never experienced such a sexualized atmosphere. Every night, everyone was going to get it on. I watched a dance floor turn into a full-blown orgy, and it seemed totally normal at the time. I did buy condoms and hand them out. I was young and didn't know that much about HIV/AIDS, but I knew more than most people, and most people in the townships weren't condomizing, as they called it. There was a common expression: "You don't eat a piece of candy with the wrapper on it."

Even though I sometimes think it's a miracle that nothing terrible happened to me that summer, it was a wonderful time. We'd wake up late on Saturdays, Banks would have some cold beers waiting for us, and we'd wander down to the football pitches and watch the weekend matches. The sun was shining, I had my flip-flops on, and I didn't have to carry a phone or a wallet or worry about where to be or what to do. I was living *loxion* style,* and I was happy.

~~~~~~

Halfway through the summer, I wrote a letter to a friend from Penn, telling her about my life in the township, my work with the students, and the deplorable lack of supplies in the schools. In particular, I told her it amazed me that none of the classrooms ever had chalk, so no one could ever write anything on the blackboards.

When my friend got the letter, she went out and bought some chalk and sent me a parcel. It arrived a week before I was due to leave the township. I took this precious box in, broke each piece into three so it would last longer, and handed them out among the students. Suddenly, the classroom came to life. Each high school student was at the board, writing out examples and drawing illustrations of his or her lessons. This one basic resource made an enormous difference in the energy of the room.

A day or two later, Banks shook me awake around 4:00 a.m. and said, "We're going for a walk." We walked across to what was known as White Location, a nearby area made up of shacks built out of salvaged materials along rutted dirt roads. As we walked closer, you could see fires burning here and there. Young girls and boys were holding rocks over the fire and, once they were hot enough, using them to iron their school uniforms.

---

* Those who lived in the townships didn't call them that—they called them locations, which got transformed into "loxion." Loxion style is laidback, taking things as they come, enjoying life.

It was one of the most powerful moments I'd ever witnessed. These kids had almost nothing, and those uniforms were often thread-bare with use, having been passed from child to child. But they took so much pride in going to school, and they wanted to look their best and be their best, even if it meant getting up at dawn to heat stones in flames. I thought to myself, *We have to keep this fire going. If we don't help these kids, it's going to burn out.*

A few days later, Banks took me to the train station, where I was meeting my friends Dan and Dan again. We were on our way to back-pack around Southern Africa for six weeks—Namibia, Angola, Zambia, Botswana, and Zimbabwe—before heading back to the United States and my final year of university. I know that Banks thought he'd never see me again; this was before cell phones or the Internet had become widespread, and the notion that we'd be able to stay in touch, much less that I'd ever come back, seemed utterly remote. As we were saying good-bye, I felt overwhelmed by what this man, a stranger in a *shebeen,* had done for me.

"How can you invite me into your home when all you know of white people is bad?" I asked. "And everywhere I go, people are so kind to me and more concerned with who I am as a person than with the color of my skin, which is not at all what I expected. What is this?"

"Jacob, it doesn't matter, the color of your skin," Banks said. "The fact that we're human beings, shouldn't that be enough that we treat each other with respect? It's what we Africans call *ubuntu.*"

CHANGING THE CONVERSATION: REDEFINING SCALE

POVERTY IS LAYERED, perpetuated by the complex interaction of many political, economic, and social challenges—government corruption, inadequate infrastructure, agricultural degradation, gendered inequality, and pervasive health care crises. It manifests itself differently around the world. A migrant worker's experience in India is fundamentally different from that of an HIV-ositive grandmother's struggle to provide for six orphans in South Africa. Yet, on the conference circuit and in the conversations throughout the development world, the focus all too often seems to be on finding a single solution for poverty. Policy makers and philanthropists spend hours discussing the challenges of combating poverty only to come to the same conclusion—something is not working. There's always a magic bullet: more aid, less aid, foreign direct investment, structural adjustments, debt forgiveness—the list goes on. These "solutions" all assume that poverty's underlying cause can be boiled down to a single obstacle.

Hand in hand with this conversation comes an insistence on "scale"—meaning, in this context, an imperative to reach as many people as possible across as many regions as possible. To make that possible, organizations focus on providing an easily replicable or easily distributable product: soup or mosquito nets, or even schools or clinics. These one-off interventions can make a difference, of course, in terms of providing something that would otherwise be missing in the community. But they disregard the sheer complexity of the poverty trap—a new school can't help a child who is being abused at home or taking care of three siblings because her parents have died of HIV-related illnesses. Without surrounding services that provide holistic support, few people will see their lives change because of single, highly scaled interventions.

What does Ubuntu do differently? We redefine "going to scale." When we had success early on with our health education services, we could have taken these services to other communities and devoted our growing fund-raising power to dramatically expanding our geographical reach. Instead, we drew a perimeter around a community of 400,000 people and provided household stability services, counseling, early childhood education. We didn't want to be an education organization or a health care organization or a nutrition organization. We wanted to provide these children with absolutely everything they needed.

We focus on depth rather than breadth; rather than incrementally benefiting

(continued)

hundreds of thousands, we strive to dramatically impact thousands of people's lives. Addressing only one facet is insufficient. Providing school supplies to an HIV-positive student who cannot afford medication is ineffective, and distributing antiretroviral drugs to food-insecure households is not enough. You must look at the whole child, at the entirety of her needs, to fundamentally change her life.

Ned Breslin is the CEO of Water for People, an international nonprofit that works with local resources to improve water and sanitation access in districts across the globe. Before joining Water for People, Breslin worked in Kenya, South Africa, Zimbabwe, and Mozambique on issues of water and sanitation. He is a 2011 recipient of the Skoll Award for Social Entrepreneurship.

Why, despite billion-dollar investments, do millions still lack access to clean water? How does this issue—water accessibility—impact their day-to-day lives?

BRESLIN: The industry narrative goes something like this: A girl in tattered clothes walks miles down a muddy path, past her school, to collect polluted water from dirty puddles. These chores, managed disproportionately by girls, strain already overburdened children, preventing many from attending school and inhibiting their ability to break the cycle of poverty.

The answer to this problem is simple, right? She needs water, so let's install a hand pump or a tap.

Yet, in reality, this girl will pass a series of rusted hand pumps and crumbling wells—reminders of broken promises—on these morning walks to fetch water. Africa, Asia, and Latin America are littered with failed water investments because they were rushed, because sustainability is not truly considered, and as such our actions—quick fixes—do not match our ambition of solving the water crisis forever. Children suffer from our negligence.

How can water-focused organizations, or any unsuccessful nonprofit for that matter, change? What does an effective, sustainable solution look like?

BRESLIN: Imagine what the outcome will be—what a world where everyone has access to water and sanitation services forever actually looks like, and build your programs from that starting point. Match your vision with audacious action and implementation, monitor for a long time to verify results, and provide hopefully declining support over time. At some point, when challenges emerge, they can be addressed fully by local leaders. Work in such a way that your nonprofit's footprint declines and eventually disappears from the scene, as you are no longer needed.

Water for People has spent more than a decade designing a model that can achieve this mission.

What does that model look like?

BRESLIN: Water for People brings together local entrepreneurs, civil society, governments, and communities to establish creative, collaborative solutions that allow people to build and maintain their own reliable, safe water systems. Empowering everyone transforms people's lives by improving health and economic productivity to end the cycle of poverty.

We collaborate with local partners to target districts in defined geographic regions managed by a local government authority, which range from 150,000 people in a district in Bolivia to almost one million people in a district in India. Financial and physical investments are then made by local and national governments, community residents, and other organizations to address current and future challenges of water systems. Water for People works with all relevant stakeholders for five years, building partnership and operational capacity to ensure that water infrastructure is managed properly. We then continue to monitor field results for ten [more] years to ensure that our programs are effective while ensuring that monitoring and evaluation capacity is firmly embedded within the beneficiary district.

Momentum builds as districts achieve full coverage, where every family, every school, and every clinic has access to reliable and safe water and sanitation services. Local leaders see the benefits of this model and reach out to partner with Water for People. They use our philanthropic investments to catalyze local financial investments, and success is achieved when everyone has access to reliable service and the district as a whole never needs another international NGO to support water and sanitation.

What does scale look like for Water for People? What can other organizations learn from your model?

BRESLIN: Scale, to Water for People, is slightly different from what it may be for other nonprofits. We are focused on modeling success at a district-wide

(continued)

scale in various countries around the world. We show how it is done in practice, and do it in a way that [allows] other local governments [to] see how it is
done and reallocate their resources and energies to achieve the same result.

This kind of positive deviance model emerged in the nutrition community
thirty to forty years ago, I believe. In Haiti, you could walk into a village that was
extremely poor, where malnutrition was rife and where challenges were abun-
dant. Yet even in these villages, there were children who thrived—[were] well
nourished, clean, at school. And when you looked at why, it was not because
of some external donor, or a family that was better placed than others. It was
that their parents took really good care of them.

So nutritionists used them to "educate" others—kind of "See, if they can
do it, then you can do it, too, as there is nothing that really differentiates
between your family and that family that is thriving." People would say, "Yep, I
can do that," or even got a bit competitive—"If they can do it, I will do it better."

We have applied the same principle at Water for People—as districts we
support achieve full water coverage, we want neighboring districts to replicate
this approach. Mayors implement it, and then they brag and say to other mayors, "Look at what I did, I am solving a key development challenge and I am
getting more money." And other mayors say, "If he can do it, so can I."

It basically shows how it is done and strips [out] all the sector jargon that
separates "experts" from people. It demonstrates what success looks like,
makes it compelling, and encourages others to say, "I can do that, too."

In today's fund-raising climate, there is an immense amount of pressure
for nonprofits to scale, and scale quickly. This environment has caused many
organizations to lose sight of their long-term missions, and I fear that the end
result will circle back to roads littered with broken water pumps. But, if we can
change this conversation and refocus on outcomes and quality programming, I
think we can certainly achieve both scale and our sector-wide goals.

**You spoke about the speed at which organizations are expected to scale
up. How long should it take a nonprofit to scale? Are there any red flags
that show that a nonprofit is trying to scale up too quickly?**

BRESLIN: At Water for People, we spend fifteen years in a district. But, when
considering the outcome of complete water accessibility, that time period
doesn't seem so long.

I think there are many signs that a nonprofit isn't ready, but there are several obvious red flags.

One is talking about a solution after very little testing, as if it is a silver bullet. So you will hear words like "breakthrough," "innovative," "scalable" . . . without much evidence to back it up.

Another involves talking about the solution as if your NGO is the only one on the planet. Water for People tested our model, but we have also "given it away" and brought others in, and we recognize that others will adopt and edit it. Good. We could have kept this "our thing" very easily. So NGOs scale too fast when they think they are the only game in town.

Third, when nonprofits start to chase money for scale—taking the attitude that we did it here and now [we] can go here and here. . . .

Lastly, when they have a delivery model that is not clear and not linked to field practice. They end up with gaps because they haven't figured it out yet.

Is there enough water for everyone? Given that we live in an increasingly water-scarce world and that climate change disproportionately affects much of the developing world, how is Water for People's model sustainable? Will your model or your ability to scale change in the coming decades?

BRESLIN: Water scarcity will be one of the biggest challenges that we face, but our mission—water for everyone, forever—remains unchanged. We are just going to have to think bigger, collaborate, and innovate. We have to develop better ways to capture, recycle, and reuse water resources so that everyone can be confident that water will flow for them forever.

CHAPTER FOUR

From HTML to HIV

THE ROOM WAS SPACIOUS, AND WINDOWS AT EITHER END MEANT THAT IT was always filled with light. The walls bore fresh coats of cheerful colors—blue, yellow, orange—a contrast to the run-down classrooms that surrounded it. And arranged on long tables around the room were more than a dozen computers, an astonishing array for Emfundweni Primary School, where few of the teachers and none of the students had any exposure to technology—there wasn't even a radio. But Banks and I were happiest to see the words painted above the door: Ubuntu Education Fund Project.

I'd left Banks at that train station in Port Elizabeth two years earlier. They were exhilarating years and exasperating years during which we'd had to teach ourselves how to build a nonprofit organization from scratch, figure out what to do with the money we did manage to raise, and channel all the time and energy we could into executing our ideas. And it had culminated in this: our first computer lab, installed in the school where Banks taught and where I'd begun working with students from the township.

Emfundweni had continued to be central to our work. The principal offered us a small storage room as the global headquarters for our fledgling organization, and we'd set up desks and filing cabinets there. When we settled on a computer lab as our first major project, it was natural that it would be located in the school.

As we geared up for this undertaking, part of the process included meeting with the entire school community: administrators, teachers, and parents. At one meeting, soon after we announced our intention to build a lab in Emfundweni, Banks, the principal and other teachers, and I were at the front of the room, sitting in the beat-up orange plastic chairs the kids used, while adults filled the room—mostly aunts and grandmothers wearing traditional head wraps and blankets, all greeting each other in Xhosa.

These meetings were the first time I realized how many children weren't being raised by their biological parents, whether because their parents had died or had left them. (It wasn't uncommon to leave sleepy Port Elizabeth for Johannesburg, "City of Gold," in pursuit of work; inevitably, after a person scraped together all her money to pay for the trip there, she'd arrive to find herself in a Johannesburg township with a million other people, no job, and no way to get back to Port Elizabeth.) The room was crowded, and hot. I still wasn't fluent in Xhosa, so I relied on Banks to translate for me. I felt pumped up with adrenaline. After all, we were on track to build an amazing computer lab. I was sure that the meeting would be in large part a celebration of Ubuntu's ambition.

And, in some ways, it was. People were thrilled: They'd asked us to help their children have access to technology, and we were going to do it. Whether these labs were a success or not didn't mean as much as the mere fact that children in this school would now have their own brand-new, high-quality computers—something that was unprecedented in the community. But something more serious was about to happen, and this meeting would change Ubuntu completely.

When I left Banks at the train station, when he told me that *ubuntu* was what had brought us together to live in that tiny apartment in the railway flats, he was convinced that that was the last he'd ever see of me, and that he'd likely never hear from me again. But two months later, after traveling all over sub-Saharan Africa and then finally heading back to the United States, I called him at the Emfundweni office. "Banks," I said over the crackling line. "What's going on with Sindi? Did the government buy books for the children?"

It became a ritual; I'd call Banks, and we'd spend hours talking about all these students that I'd met over the summer, and brainstorming ways that we could smooth their path to a better future. Banks had a lot of energy, and a lot of patience, but even he would be flagging by the end of some of those conversations. I felt like I was on fire.

I'd returned to Penn a changed person. When I thought about sitting in a classroom talking about theories of history and development, I felt both restless and frustrated. How could I sit around when I knew I could be doing something to help these kids? Somehow, I convinced Dr. Berry to support an independent study project that gave me most of the credits I needed to graduate, letting me work on launching what Banks and I decided to call Ubuntu Education Fund. (When I told Dr. Berry what had happened over the summer, she said a bit dismissively, "Oh, you got inspired. So what are you going to do now?" She always supported me and offered great guidance, but I'm sure that to a civil rights activist, I looked like just another young kid whose passion would fade as the experience of living in the townships receded into the past.)

I lived in a house with seven friends and, as I began recruiting help for this new organization, they became the early volunteer corps, along with a few others. I'd met one volunteer, a sophomore named Lindsay, a few days earlier. I'd approached her because she was wearing a Maine T-shirt, and I told her she should come to my volunteer meeting. Next to me in the meeting was Dan Friedland, who had been in South Africa at the same time I had been. In our many conversations about the townships and Ubuntu, he'd always encouraged me to move forward, and his creativity and energy made him an ideal partner in this young venture. I stood up and said, "This is going to be a lot of work, but here's what needs to happen. We need to design a Web site, we need to come up with letterhead, we need to send letters to every person you know asking for money."

We started off with a raffle to raise the money to buy office supplies: printer cartridges, stationery with our logo on it, and stamps. Somehow, someone got me a copy of the address list for parents with children currently enrolled at Penn, and we used that list, along with every person we knew, for our first mass fund-raising mailing. We put together a brochure that described the goals of Ubuntu:

1. *To supply each classroom of Emfundweni and Ndzondelelo with pencils, chalk, notebooks, dictionaries, and maps.*

2. *To supply each classroom with Math and Science Kits. These are packages of standardized resources that are essential in preparing a class to pass the national examinations.*

3. *To fund and construct the Irving Lief Library at the Ndzondelelo Secondary School, a resource for the entire community.*

4. *To expand Ubuntu Education Fund support to include other township schools.*

I also wrote up a letter describing what we were doing, and then we divvied all of them up and wrote personal notes on each one. We sent out 449 letters before we ran out of money for postage. When we finally dropped the stacks of envelopes into the mailbox, the anticipation was so pitched it was difficult to bear—excitement that this stage was past, and fear that nothing would come of it.

As we started to get responses back, each one we opened offered a little more encouragement. We got many checks for $25 or $50, and a few donated a few hundred dollars. In the end, we raised $8,000. When we totaled it up, I called Banks with the news. We started excitedly planning what we could do with the money—a fax machine for Emfundweni! Toys for the kindergartners! Chalk for all the classrooms!

Even before we'd started to get donations back, I'd begun thinking about the next step with Ubuntu. It was the spring of my senior year, and I had to make some decisions about what I was going to do after graduation. At the time, starting a nonprofit organization and pursuing social entrepreneurship wasn't a common career choice for a new university graduate, and when I talked about continuing with Ubuntu as my career, people looked at me like I was crazy. I did what every other senior did that spring and filled out a questionnaire for career services. You told them what languages you spoke, what job experience you had, and what you hoped to do following graduation, and they were supposed to call you to talk about resources and advice. I wrote down "Xhosa," "Started a tutoring program in a South African township," and "Start Ubuntu." No one ever called me.

But despite the naysayers, I knew it was what I wanted to do. I was going to start Ubuntu with Banks, and we were going to take one little corner of the world and change it.

~~~~~~~

Two days after graduation, I got in my car with my friend Dan Byrd (who'd visited me in the townships, along with Dan Friedland), and spent seven weeks driving across Canada and up through Alaska to the Arctic Ocean. All we had were sleeping bags, fishing rods, and a tent. Throughout the quiet solitude of that trip—hiking into the backcountry, fishing for our supper every night—I thought about Port Elizabeth, the children in the townships, and Ubuntu. By the time we made it back to the East Coast, I had put together a plan in my mind for our nascent organization.

The first step was to disburse all the money we'd raised. I bought a ticket to South Africa and got on the plane with $8,000 in cash tucked in my carry-on bag. I'd been completely disconnected during my trip north, so I was filled with anxiety: How would the township have changed? Would they even need this help? When I arrived, nothing had changed at all since the morning I'd boarded the train out of Port Elizabeth. It could have been the next day. Banks greeted me effusively at the airport, and we set out to spend the money.

Banks and I were like two kids in a toy store on an unlimited shopping spree. We wanted to buy Emfundweni and Ndzondelelo every teaching aid you can imagine, from workbooks to mathematical games to calculators—everything. I spent eight days in Port Elizabeth. At the end of it, I looked at Banks and felt empty. I said, "Is this what it's all about?" Those educational resources weren't going to help; they were going to break, whether tomorrow or two years from now. I'd fallen prey to the same handout syndrome I'd seen fail so many times. It was everything that I knew was wrong about development.

Banks and I decided that the next step was to raise some money so we could canvass the township, spend six months talking to as many people as we could, meeting with the schools and the parents, the grannies and the aunts, and figure out not what we *could* do, but what we *needed* to do. Suddenly, what had seemed relatively straightforward—raise money, spend money—had new complexity.

I was excited to get back and tell Dan Friedland, my partner running Ubuntu in the United States, all about the trip and how it had hit me that we needed to do more than buy material things for the schools. But when I saw him, he said, "I just never thought we'd actually do it." He didn't feel the same passion I did, and once we both realized it, it was clearly time to move in different directions. So he left Ubuntu to start to figure out what he wanted to do with the rest of his life.

I was crushed. Dan had been an essential part of starting Ubuntu. He wrote most of our communications materials, he'd found a nonprofit incubator called Resources for Human Development that helped launch us, and we brainstormed together constantly. But I'd never thought we wouldn't do it, and I couldn't even imagine not thinking we would. I'd put on the blinders of a true believer, and it caused me to develop an intolerance for doubt. I didn't talk to him for many years because I felt, in some way, betrayed—especially because Dan had been integral to Ubuntu during our first months.

Now, of course, I realize that I put him in an unfair position. I wanted a partner, but he could never have the same energy for Ubuntu as I did; I'd lived in the townships, with the people we were working with, and he hadn't. And that made all the difference.

After a summer traveling, and then the trip to South Africa, I had no money to rent an apartment in Philadelphia. So I moved in with my parents in Maine and got a job clearing land of trees and brush. In the evenings I wrote grant proposals. Eventually, I got a $2,500 grant from a family foundation in Beeville, Texas, called the James R. Dougherty Jr. Foundation. I don't know where I found them, I've had no contact with them since, and to this day I have no idea why they supported us, but the grant gave me the confidence to quit my job clearing land.

I decided to move back to Philadelphia. Lindsay and I had been dating seriously for a year by this point, and I wanted to be near her while she finished university. So, in December of 1999, for $300 a month, I rented a tiny apartment where I had to wash my dishes in the bathtub. I also had a tiny office with no windows, where I'd go each morning, close the door, and have no idea what to do. The loneliness swamped me. Back in Port Elizabeth, Banks was out talking to people, using his connections in the community to develop a map for the future. He was truly engaged. But I was in charge of strategy and fund-raising, and I had no one to talk to. At that point, I didn't even have an e-mail address.

Most people I knew viewed what I was doing with a mixture of amusement and condescension. "Oh, good for you, you're so idealistic! Good luck with this Africa project." They saw it as a dilettante's effort, something I'd dabble in for a couple of years until I woke up and got a consulting job or went to law school like everyone else. The exception, and the one that made the biggest difference for me, was my parents. They always supported and encouraged me.

I learned never to be shy about exploiting a connection, or asking for a favor. Through friends, Ubuntu got its first big media profile, in the Newark, New Jersey, *Star-Ledger*. Then my father showed the article to a lawyer he was doing business with in New York, Bill Voge, who was a partner at Latham and Watkins. Bill asked, "Does he have legal counsel?" We didn't, so he arranged to meet with me. When I got to his office, he said, "I've got to be straight with you. Most people who start these organizations never carry through. They realize how hard it is and quit." He was testing my dedication. By the end of that meeting, I'd convinced him. He handed me a check, which in those days was always huge for us, and agreed to represent us pro bono. Most important, he gave me invaluable advice about knowing your worth. He said, "I want to be clear that even though this will be pro bono advice, you'll have access to a partner, which is me, and you'll have access to an associate. Don't ever accept pro bono services or in-kind services if they don't treat you the same way they would treat a paying client."

The grant from the James R. Dougherty Jr. Foundation marked the one success in a stack of rejection letters from the most famous names in the foundation world: Ford, Carnegie, Rockefeller. I was living in Philadelphia, getting to New York City whenever I could and meeting with anyone I could, but very few wanted to meet with me. The frustration had built to a breaking point. My mother, who had worked for an incredible organization called Ashoka, arranged a meeting with Bill Drayton, its founder. He helped popularize the term "social entrepreneurship," and his organization supports such entrepreneurs around the globe. He reminds me a bit of Bill Gates, both in appearance— he's wiry and intelligent looking, with a well-tamed mop of hair and glasses—and in the way that he fundamentally revolutionized his field. Bill said, "Okay, meet me at the Algonquin Hotel in Midtown. I'm taking a taxi down to Wall Street, and you can ride with me and pick my brain."

The first thing I did was show him all my rejection letters. He looked through them and shook his head. He told me to forget about the foundations and concentrate on wealthy individuals for now: They might be harder to identify, because they aren't public, but they're unrestricted money. And to win over an individual, sometimes all you have to do is show them a picture of cute children. For nonprofits, grants often come with strings attached: The money must be used for whatever program the foundation wants to support, and only a low ratio can be spent on what is considered overhead, including staff salaries. With unrestricted money, an organization is given the freedom to decide where they need to put the funds, and you're not required to report how those specific dollars were spent. "Build your unrestricted donor base," Bill said. "After three years, you'll have a track record, and then you can start looking for funding through grants." To this day, that's the best advice I've ever received about starting a nonprofit.

~~~~~

Still, I'd become impatient with the slow pace of fund-raising and wanted to get back to South Africa and start doing something. We had a few supporters, like Bill Voge, who gave us generous donations, but we needed more money. At university, credit cards seemed to be given out like candy, and I'd amassed nine of them. They became an easy way to pay for the shortfall between our donations and our operating expenses. I ran up $23,000 in debt.

In early 2000, I flew to South Africa to help Banks canvass the township. What did people want for their children? What was the most pressing need in the schools? We attended meeting after meeting with families in rundown classrooms or crowded into shacks. We believed in community buy-in, so we had to be sure that the whole community was involved in our work. Through hundreds of hours of conversation, we heard that while these children were the first generation to have equal access to the university system in South Africa, they didn't have the training in technology to compete. How can a kid who has never even seen a desktop computer get into, much less survive, a university environment in which everything, from course registration to exams, gets done on computers? It was an easy decision: Our first project, Sivulile ("Opening Doors"), would be to build a computer center.

It couldn't have gone better. From the time we decided on a computer center at Emfundweni to the moment it was completed, everything worked. Part of it was that Banks and I were so enthusiastic that we went in with guns blazing. Paint the room? We can do that! Get custom desks built? No problem! Every obstacle felt like part of the excitement.

And it did turn out great, in many ways. We took an old staff room, where the windows were broken and the doors rusted, and repaired everything. We painted the walls rainbow colors, put new glass in the windows and hung curtains, and fixed the doors. Along the walls we set up long desks, which held fifteen new computers and five laser printers. We were full of optimism, convinced that this was the start of amazing things.

~~~~~~

On a cool July morning of 2000, the computer center was finally complete. We had a big opening planned: the mayor, the principal, and Banks and I all planned to speak. Some of the grannies in the school had made me an *isikaka,* a flowing shirt and pants that, paired with my long hair, made me look like a South African Jesus Christ. Banks insisted I wear it as a sign of respect to the women of the school community.

A huge crowd, close to a thousand men, women, and children, poured into the school's courtyard. Our guest of honor, the mayor of Port Elizabeth, had not yet shown up. The minutes passed: Fifteen minutes, half an hour, a full hour went by, with no sign of and no word from the mayor's office. The wind was blowing hard, and we all had to squint against the dust that blew in our eyes. Finally, I lost my temper. I took the lectern and began speaking. "We are all gathered here to celebrate this great new computer room. I wanted your mayor here, the one you voted in. But apparently he didn't have the time to show up. What do you think he's doing that is so important?"

I took several deep breaths, and then went on with the speech I'd written so carefully. This was a joyful occasion, and I wanted not only to mark our accomplishment but also to inspire the community to keep working with us, to keep aiming for more and better: "Let us look at this computer center for what it really is. It is merely one brick. The center will not solve our problems . . . for one brick is not a house."

As I finished my speech, a young man made his way to the front and pulled me aside. "Oh, yes, the mayor is coming," he assured me. Fifteen minutes later, the mayor arrived and gave his speech, as though he'd intended to be there all along. The next day, a few members of his inner circle paid a visit to Banks and me in our tiny office and let us know that if we wanted to keep working in Port Elizabeth, we better not do anything like that again. The message came through clearly: Don't even think about calling out the mayor.

When they left, Banks shook his head at me. "See, Jake. You have to handle these things at the right time." To this day, I struggle with this aspect of working in South Africa—the careful, roundabout way of dealing with problems—and tend to bluntly point out when people are wrong. And it still sometimes gets me in trouble. Banks has a temper worse than mine, but he is sometimes better about knowing the time and place to express it. I knew Banks was right, but at the same time, the mayor *had* shown up.

~~~~~~

Now we were looking to the next project. We wanted to get computers into other schools, and we also wanted to start building libraries in the schools, so children could access books without having to walk to the township library. I was out fund-raising, with a goal of doubling the amount we'd brought in during the previous year.

I quickly learned that certain phrases or pieces of data elicited a strong response from donors. For instance, I talked a lot in these days about "technological apartheid," urging people to bridge the digital divide in the same way that they had brought down the National Party government. We were combating this "technological apartheid" with our computer centers. It's the sort of phrase that now makes me cringe, jargon that sounds impressive but doesn't actually mean a whole lot. I'd also emphasize to donors that we were aiming to reach forty thousand children through our programs. I was obsessed with that number. I was newly out of university, it sounded impressive to me, and it worked: People heard "forty thousand," they felt like it made us credible, and they gave us money. The problem was that forty thousand was based on outputs. Yes, we would reach forty thousand—through the computer center and others like it that we were planning, through the libraries we were setting out to build. But those centers were just places. What we weren't talking about was how many children were now computer literate. That's an actual outcome, but that's harder to achieve, and harder to quantify.

That hit home after we opened the Emfundweni computer center and realized that building it had been the easy part. We had invested a large chunk of money in training the teachers; after all, most of them had had as little exposure to technology as their students. But people didn't attend the courses regularly, and we were spending a lot of time running the center because there wasn't anyone at the school who could do it. People were excited to have this shiny, state-of-the-art center in their local school, but they fell into the trap of thinking that's all you needed, and now everyone would go to university. There's a lot of work that needs to be done to make that happen, and the school and the teachers weren't prepared to do it.

More important, even as students used the computer lab and started to become more proficient in using the technology, clearly it wasn't changing their lives. For an hour a day, they were getting training for the future. But for twenty-three hours of the day, they were fighting just to survive, and any future seemed more like a dream than a potential reality.

~~~~~~

At times, it was easy to lose sight of that bigger picture, but our community always brought it back into focus. At that late summer meeting in Port Elizabeth, when we'd gathered with the school principal and teachers for a meeting, we began with celebration. The room was packed, and when the principal started the meeting by announcing that we'd be building a computer center in Emfundweni, the room burst into joyful song. The reaction was phenomenal, and I couldn't help but have a little jolt of self-satisfaction. As the crowd started to settle back down, a woman stood up and began speaking in Xhosa. I could tell that she was speaking about something new, and quite serious. The principal shifted in his seat uncomfortably. I leaned over to Banks and asked, "What's going on?"

Banks told me that she had said, "This is all wonderful, but three children this year have died of this thing called AIDS. What are we going to do about that?" I felt as though the floor dropped out from under me. Suddenly, bridging the "digital divide," putting in computers to combat "technological apartheid"—these weren't the keys to success. What good was a computer to a dying child?

HIV and AIDS were inescapable in the townships: In 2000, when we opened the computer center, more than four million people were infected with HIV in South Africa (out of a population of forty million), and, in the townships of Port Elizabeth, more than 40 percent of residents were HIV-positive. Yet, no one really talked about it. The South African government denied that there was a proven connection between HIV and AIDS and promoted treatment with herbal remedies rather than antiretroviral drugs. People claimed that the virus came from Coca-Cola, from imported oranges, that it only affected gay people; to cure it, they said you should sleep with a virgin, take a shower after sex, eat traditional foods. No one wanted to use condoms.

The next day, Banks and I drove to the Red Cross in Port Elizabeth, the only health organization working in the city. Four of their volunteers became the first staff of our health intervention program, Mpilo-Lwazi ("health knowledge").

Implementing a curriculum wasn't easy. Banks and I didn't know what we were doing, so it was an intense learning process. We started by going into the schools to have workshops, teaching the children about prevention. But of course it wasn't as though everyone was suddenly comfortable discussing it, or immediately convinced that the information we were providing was right. Even among our staff, it was a struggle. You'd hear about a young person, twenty-nine years old, who'd died, clearly because of HIV/AIDS. But people would say, "Oh, he was feverish."

On the weekends, social life consisted of attending funerals, which took place all day on Saturday and Sunday. There'd be a traditional church service, the burial, and then the family would slaughter an animal and provide a meal. Huge cemeteries in the townships closed because there was no more space. After a while, you wondered if the constant reminders of death, the way that funerals consumed every weekend, had begun to devalue life in some way.

That woman at the parents' meeting changed the course of our organization. Ubuntu was no longer about setting a goal—to build a computer center, say, or raise $200,000—and accomplishing it; this was a matter of life or death. I was twenty-two years old, and suddenly I felt responsible for the lives of thousands of children and adults. I had no training, no preparation for this. But now that we realized what was necessary, there was no choice but to do it.

CHANGING THE CONVERSATION: EMBRACING BOTTOM-UP DEVELOPMENT

SO MUCH IS right about grassroots organizations: They understand the communities they work in, they involve local leadership in their programs, and they tend to be in it for the long haul because they have meaningful ties to the places where they work. But more often than not, these organizations, which are doing important, valuable work, end up stymied. They don't have the resources or the ability to operate in a more professional way—to strategize, to budget, to forecast what their operational needs will be in a year. I think of the grandmother in Zwide who keeps all her money in her bra and has twenty orphans living in her garage; it's an extreme but vivid example of the level of impact being stunted by a lack of capacity. Of course, she's doing something invaluable for the kids she takes in, but she's also limited in her ability to grow.

From the beginning, Ubuntu has placed the community at the center of its own development. Much of Ubuntu's evolution as an organization occurred directly as a result of community members' input—from building computer centers to providing HIV/AIDS education to the construction of the Ubuntu Centre. But most important, we invest heavily in our staff. We hire 95 percent of our employees from the community in which we work. We've recognized over the years that passion, professionalism, and cultural literacy far outweigh a paper-perfect resume. We look for raw talent and, with BUILD (Bertha–Ubuntu Internal Leadership Development), our staff development initiative, provide our team with the tools to learn and grow within the organization.

The best companies in the world thrive in part because they invest in hiring, training, and retaining their employees, and that's what Ubuntu does. That means everything from giving them free coffee to stipends for further education, from yoga to competitive salaries and health insurance. It isn't revolutionary, but it is unusual in the nonprofit world, and especially for a nonprofit that still operates with a grassroots mind-set. We're a part of the fabric of the community, and our success as an organization is dependent on its thriving. This symbiosis allows us to be flexible, to recognize issues on the ground quickly and respond sensitively, and to adapt over time as the community changes. But we've professionalized this grassroots service-delivery model, melded bottom-up development to global best practices in hiring, accounting, and transparency. That's how you build long-term sustainability.

(continued)

Daniel Lurie is a San Francisco–based philanthropist whose group, Tipping Point Community, provides financial and capacity-building grants to grassroots organizations in the Bay Area that fight poverty. Since 2005, Tipping Point has raised more than $80 million and reached more than 365,000 people in need. While depending on data and benchmarks to assess and monitor the groups it funds, Tipping Point also provides expert help, from partners such as Hewlett-Packard and Charles Schwab, to improve leadership and performance. Before founding Tipping Point, Lurie worked for Bill Bradley's 2000 presidential campaign, Accenture, and the Robin Hood Foundation. He also serves on the boards of directors of the Mimi and Peter Haas Fund, the Levi Strauss Foundation, and Single Stop USA and is the chair of the San Francisco Bay Area Super Bowl 50 Host Committee.

Why should we invest in community-based, grassroots organizations? What do they bring to the table?

LURIE: Community organizations and the leaders within them have a deep understanding of local contexts that we, as funders, simply cannot learn in a yearlong grant cycle. These leaders bring an expertise grounded in a lifetime of daily interactions with the challenges that they aim to mitigate. They know if there are potholes in the elementary school parking lot or that the fence is broken outside the women's shelter. They are always on, poring over spreadsheets to stretch limited resources, networking with potential donors, and devising solutions to seemingly endless challenges. This familiarity informs their programmatic models and, with the support of smart investments in their vision, ultimately results in more effective, practical solutions.

What obstacles do these nonprofits face? Why are they sometimes overlooked?

LURIE: Many small nonprofits have limited time, resources, and funding. Some operate on shoestring budgets, or equip staff with donated, ten-year-old computers. One employee might bear the workload of five people but get compensated far less than an entry-level corporate associate. Consequently, these organizations can never think ahead—there is immediacy to every aspect of the work and a constant threat of an empty bank account. This funding shortfall and survival-mode mentality impedes their ability to do their best work and makes it difficult to implement new strategies or improve existing ones. Unable either to prove their impact or expand, small nonprofits unfairly garner a reputation of being inefficient and unsuccessful.

How can we empower community-based organizations?

LURIE: We first must begin to view the funder/grantee relationship as one of partnership. As it stands, donors are often skeptical of organizations' overhead and reporting, and put an immense amount of pressure on scalability. Many make short-term investments and provide little insight into grant-making decisions. Nonprofits, in turn, feel that they cannot always be honest with funders. If any number of factors leads to unexpected results, grantees feel the need to skirt around the details to avoid a potential loss of funding. Moreover, they may not feel supported to take risks to make bigger gains for fear of perceived failure. This dynamic is unhealthy. Not only does it undermine accountability but also it inhibits nonprofits and funders from pooling resources and knowledge to effect real change. If funders can reframe this relationship as one of long-term partnership, I believe we can encourage honesty and work with grassroots organizations to build capacity, strengthen impact, and achieve great outcomes.

What other long-term investments would you encourage funders to make in nonprofits?

LURIE: As philanthropists, we need to recognize that organizations are only as efficient as the people who run them. Funders need to invest in general operating costs, and in supporting key infrastructural projects ranging from technology upgrades to staff development. We have to recruit talented employees to our sector, provide them with the proper training, and empower them to implement programs effectively.

What do you look for in a grassroots organization before investing?

LURIE: At Tipping Point Community, we look for two main things: visionary leadership and a commitment to absolute honesty. We spend about one hundred hours in due diligence per organization before we write a check. In this screening process, we assess each organization's financials, willingness to engage with a deeply involved funder like us, and use of data to improve the

(continued)

model and outcomes. We try to find CEOs whose visions align with the way we run our own organization—those who are truly willing to take a hard look at their model from top to bottom, want to keep learning and growing, and thrive on open communication and feedback.

Can you give an example of a grassroots organization that Tipping Point has worked with successfully?

LURIE: We often use the example of Year Up to illustrate Tipping Point's impact. Founded in 2000 on the East Coast, Year Up is a national nonprofit that serves low-income and disconnected young people between the ages of eighteen and twenty-four. In its intensive one-year program, participants receive six months of technical and professional training followed by a six-month internship at a local partner company. Tipping Point made an initial investment in Year Up to seed its efforts in the Bay Area. On top of the more than two million in general operating dollars that Tipping Point has granted to Year Up, we've also provided staff training and support on events and communications, connected the organization to resources in the areas of human capital and mental health services, and facilitated introductions to additional funding sources to ensure its long-term success in the Bay Area. Within four months of graduating from the program, 91 percent of Year Up graduates are either employed or enrolled in community college full-time.

What drew you to work with these kinds of organizations?

LURIE: After I finished college, I moved to New York City and started working for the Robin Hood Foundation, an organization focused on fighting poverty. September 11, 2001, happened during my first week of work at Robin Hood. I actually saw the first plane hit the World Trade tower as I came up from the subway on Broadway. It's an image I will never forget. That tragedy was an extremely difficult time for everyone, all across the country. And for the next two years, I got to be part of the team at Robin Hood as we worked to help lift up those hardest hit by the attacks. Robin Hood's efforts were so effective in rebuilding the city after September 11th that I immediately knew the Bay Area needed something like that, too. More than a million people living here in the Bay Area struggle to meet their basic needs; they choose between putting food on the table and paying the rent. We couldn't wait for a tragedy like September 11th to come together as a community.

CHAPTER FIVE

The Already-
Colored-In
Coloring Book

At the end of one of my visits to Port Elizabeth—by late 2000, I was traveling back and forth between Philadelphia and South Africa eight times a year—Banks decided to throw a huge *braai*. We did this a lot at the time, because it was a way to finish off a long day and to rejuvenate our staff, to give people who weren't being paid a lot a treat. Understand, a *braai* isn't just a barbecue. It transcends racial and socio-economic lines. It's a South African national pastime. Every apartment, every house, every little shack, has somewhere where you *braai*. Every butcher in the townships has a place out back where you can *braai* your meat. Every tavern has space to *braai*. A *braai* consists of much more than cooking the meat and eating, of course. It can encompass the whole evening, or even an entire day.

When I lived with Banks in the railway flats, we'd hosted some legendary *braais*. One day, I went out on a commercial fishing boat with a friend who was visiting and caught a shark. I brought it back with me; no one had ever seen anything like it. So, naturally, we decided to *braai* it, and it turned into an all-night event of drinking and carving off huge slabs of shark meat for the grill.

Most of all, I love how the *braai* reflects and reinforces community bonds. When you *braai* the Xhosa way, you cook the meat, then you cut it into pieces and pass it around and everyone takes a piece, and keeps passing until it's gone. As the head of an organization, you are constantly thinking about how to build trust and morale. For Ubuntu, the *braai* did all that.

At this *braai*, we were celebrating the opening of several new computer centers, and Banks had invited all the teachers from the schools we were working in, along with our staff. There's a saying in the township that "once you see the smoke, you're invited," so even more people showed up, including a teacher named Gcobani Zonke. He'd grown up in New Brighton, a few streets away from Banks (he remembers Banks at the time: "He was a player on the local football team, and I supported it"). He taught math and science at Sivuyiseni Intermediate School, a school that, though it was located in a more middle-class area of the townships, served predominately students from the worst areas. Gcobani had heard about the work Ubuntu was doing and had begun calling Banks to see if there was something he could do to help, hoping that Ubuntu would consider working in his school. When he heard about the *braai*, Gcobani figured it might be a good opportunity to continue to press his case. I noticed him because he spent all evening tending the *braai*—usually a job for one of the younger men. After watching him at this job for hours, I went over to talk to him. He's a big guy with an open, affable expression, and we fell easily into a long conversation. He talked about his work as a teacher, and how he admired what we were doing at Ubuntu. Finally, he said, "I'd like to start volunteering for you."

This was an unusual offer. The culture of volunteerism doesn't exist in the township. After the end of apartheid, the idea of working without pay felt too close to the virtual slavery that had existed for so long. So I told Gcobani, "I'm sorry, we don't pay a stipend"—that's usually what people meant when they talked about volunteering.

"Oh, no, that's fine," Gcobani responded. "I'll just come in, and see where I can help out."

He started dropping in soon after, usually for an hour in the morning before school started, and then after school for a few hours. After a while, we asked him to join us officially as educational advisor, and he began to audit the way our life skills classes were being taught. These were classes where we were doing everything from teaching little kids about their bodies and basic health information to counseling teenagers about sex and HIV/AIDS. Gcobani had been doing teacher training for years, and he transformed our health educators' pedagogical approach. To me, Gcobani exemplifies *ubuntu*—his kindness and compassion are boundless. And that informed the way he trained teachers: Treat every student with humanity, dignity, and respect above all.

One day, Gcobani accompanied one of the educators to Dora Nginza hospital, where they visited a specific ward—Ward D. There were hundreds of people waiting there, from young mothers with babies to toddlers and teenagers to grandmothers and grandfathers. Throughout the presentation, the educator referred to them all as HIV-positive, and later, when Gcobani gave his feedback, he started by telling her not to assume that anyone is positive. His number one rule in reaching out was to provide advice and information without reference to anyone's status.

The educator looked at him levelly and said, "Everyone on that ward is positive."

As Gcobani told me later, "Suddenly, in my mind I saw a massive grave, and all those people, that little child and that beautiful girl and that old woman, all of them were going to go in this massive grave."

"It was a turning point for me," he added. "I knew I'd commit myself to any organization that talked about this dreadful virus."

~~~~~~~

Back in the United States, raising money continued to go slowly. In an effort to give us a jump-start, my mother and father offered to host our first fund-raiser in their apartment in Manhattan, where they'd recently moved. We made the simple invitations ourselves: a photo of our new computer lab, a quote from Nelson Mandela ("Children are the rock on which our future will be built. . . . "), and an offer to provide more information about South Africa and Ubuntu.

Banks flew to New York a few days before the fund-raiser, in October 2000; it was only the second time he'd been on a plane. He'd written a long speech that touched on his experiences growing up in South Africa, what Ubuntu was doing in the townships, and what we planned to do. I picked him up at the airport. He was totally exhausted from the flight; he'd never gone overseas before, and the jet lag had nailed him. Still, as we drove into Manhattan, he marveled at the skyline—at the height of the buildings, how many there were, how closely they nestled together. Soon after arriving at my parents' apartment, we went out for a walk. It was hard to tell what was hitting him harder at this point, the jet lag or the culture shock. The swarms of people on the sidewalks and the way you could feel the subway rumbling under your feet disconcerted him. And yet he hadn't quite absorbed that this was no longer the township, where people greeted each other on the streets. "Hey, Jake," he asked me at one point during our walk, "when we go to Philadelphia, will you introduce me to Will Smith?"

"Banks, I don't know him, I can't introduce you," I said, laughing a little. He looked surprised, and then he got angry with me for holding out on him.

"Can't we go knock on his door?" he asked indignantly.

When we got back to the apartment, I offered Banks a glass of fresh-squeezed grapefruit juice—my favorite. Banks had never tried it before, and he loved it. He drank glass after glass; my mother worriedly told him, "It's going to hurt your stomach. You might want to slow down." He managed to drink an entire gallon jug of the juice; unsurprisingly, he spent the rest of the day in bed.

The day of the fund-raiser came, though, and Banks and I psyched each other up to speak in front of this crowd. The whole evening turned into a blur of introductions and intense conversations. I wanted to talk to every person there about why they should support our work, and I think I succeeded. I spent some time talking to Rob Kaplan, a vice chairman at Goldman Sachs, who'd worked with my father for twenty years. As the evening drew to a close, he took me aside and said, "I want to give you seed money. Call my office and set up an appointment to talk."

A few days later, I made my way to 85 Broad Street, Goldman's headquarters at the time. I was scared and nervous, and wired on caffeine: I'd had five cups of coffee so I'd be sharp. I had on what I thought looked professional—khaki pants and a blue V-neck sweater—but I'm sure I looked foolish. I sat in the waiting room, palms sweating, until Rob's secretary ushered me in. He was eating his lunch, and though he seemed to only be half paying attention, I could tell he heard every minute of my pitch. When I'd finished, he said, "Okay, I'm going to give you $75,000—to help you get on your feet."

That was the donation that truly changed Ubuntu. Between Rob's donation and the other money we'd raised that evening, we now had about $100,000 to sustain us, and to continue to grow.

~~~~~~~

One day in the summer of 2001, I got a phone call from my friend Jordan Levy. We'd been best friends since we were four; my mom took me over to his house one day, and he burst out the door in Superman Underoos and a cape, and nothing else. We were inseparable from that day on. When my family moved to London, we didn't have the same daily interaction, but when we'd see each other during the summers, it was like we'd never been apart. We had a connection that transcended all distance.

I'd sent Jordan a letter during the summer when I was living with Banks, describing the townships and the children I was working with. It made a big impression on him. It had to have been the first letter I'd ever written him, and suddenly I was telling him, in what he remembers as an articulate and thoughtful manner, about serious issues of poverty and abuse. He'd spent two years in Spain with his girlfriend, Jana, after graduating from university, and now they were both back in the United States looking for jobs. He'd majored in international relations and political science and had a burgeoning interest in development work, so he called me.

At the time, Ubuntu had gained some momentum, and it felt like we were taking off, but we still didn't have a lot of money to cover staff salaries. We were working out of a small office space in Hoboken, New Jersey, which Tom Jaffe, a real estate developer, had donated. I'd met Tom, who became the first chairman of our board, at our second fundraiser, which was hosted by Stuart Litwin, our first board member and my first cousin, and his wife, Laura. It made a big difference to be so much closer to New York City, where we did almost all of our fundraising. Lindsay and I were both living in Manhattan; she'd recently graduated from Penn and become Ubuntu's second US staff member. I asked Jordan if he'd be interested in working for us, basically for beer. Amazingly, he said yes.

Jordan started with us on September 3, 2001. Eight days later, Jordan and I had just arrived at the office when Tom Jaffe walked in and said that a plane had hit the World Trade Center. At nearly the same moment, Lindsay called me. That morning she was scheduled to have a meeting a few blocks from the towers. She said, "What should I do? Should I still go to this meeting?" At that point, we thought it was a freak accident. So I told her to go—"They're waiting for you, it's a business meeting, you need to go."

Tom said, "Let's go to the roof." Hoboken sits right across the river, and we could see Lower Manhattan perfectly from the roof of the office building. Not long after we got up there, the second plane hit, and it was clear that this was much more than a horrible accident. I tried calling Lindsay, but I couldn't get through to her; eighteen hours passed before I had any idea if she was safe, or where she was. We watched in disbelief as the towers fell.

It took us some time to emerge from the devastation, though we had to keep working: We didn't have enough money to quit fund-raising. It was difficult, not only to stay motivated but also to convince people in New York, who were still in mourning over the attacks, to donate to an organization based in South Africa. Luckily, we knew a couple, Patrick and Margaret Grace, who pledged enough money to keep us covered for the interim. Lindsay felt traumatized by her experience on September 11—as I'd told her to do, she'd continued to her meeting downtown, only to have to take shelter as the towers collapsed. Shaken and covered in dust, she walked all the way back up to 87th Street, so in shock that it didn't even occur to her to try to reach me. In the following days, though, she kept coming out to Hoboken to work.

It wasn't the easiest experience for Jordan, because Lindsay and I both have very strong personalities and express our opinions loudly. And Lindsay's first reaction to Jordan was "Who is this guy? He doesn't even know how to open an Excel spreadsheet." We commuted from Manhattan together in the mornings. I had a Jeep that had only two seats, so Lindsay and I would sit up front and Jordan would sit in the back with whatever junk I'd thrown back there. One Monday morning, I told Jordan, "Hey, I got you a present!" He opened up the back, and there was a Mets seat cushion—I'd gone to a game over the weekend, and they were giving them out. For a guy making $200 a week, it was as close as you get to an employee benefit.

The three of us worked incredibly hard. It was as though we'd found ourselves in the Wild West of nonprofit work. The office was in the Hoboken housing projects, and we had to climb the fire escape to get in. We were doing everything ourselves, writing grant proposals, trying to find new donors, putting together publicity materials. And we certainly didn't have the best equipment or the greatest supply closet full of all the things you needed to run a business. We had one gigantic laptop that we shared. If Lindsay or Jordan wrote something down on a piece of paper, made a mistake, and then tried to throw out an entire sheet of paper, I'd get mad at them. We had so little to work with, every scrap was precious. All the while, I spent hundreds of hours on the phone with Banks, putting together a strategy for our next project. We didn't have a real plan for how to make Ubuntu work, but we were young and figured we could work intense, twelve- or fourteen-hour days, go home and drink a few beers, and then get up and do it again.

We all thrived on the feeling that we were making something out of nothing. Jordan and I already had an incredible friendship. I can't think of anyone else who would have put up with me the way Jordan did and still be willing to stick around. The trust in and real love we have for each other made a huge difference in the way we worked, and continue to work, together.

<hr />

About seven weeks after September 11, Lindsay and I left to travel for a few months before heading to South Africa for four months. After that fall, we needed a little distance to recover and figure out what we needed to do next. Lindsay had never been to South Africa for an extended period of time, and I wanted her to experience the townships the way I had. I knew Jordan was smart, I knew he was capable, and so even though he'd been there only a short time, I left him in charge of the US side of Ubuntu. He had two major tasks ahead of him: Organize a benefit, and register our organization in the thirty-four states in which we did our fund-raising. Now, either one of those easily could have been a full-time job. But in addition, Jordan was managing the payroll. (For some reason, we still couldn't manage this from Port Elizabeth—one of the strange inefficiencies of a start-up.)

In my mind, I'd thoroughly trained Jordan, but we'd never had a conversation or reviewed how, exactly, he was supposed to get all this stuff done. He had to find 345 people to attend our first big-time fund-raising event, an off-Broadway play called *Syringa Tree,* but he didn't know anyone who made money; I told him, "Just call everybody on our donor list and badger them until they buy a ticket." (Jordan managed to get 330 people to attend, then the largest fund-raising event we'd hosted, and we raised $38,000 that evening.)

Every week, the South Africa office would call with a list of names and salaries for the payroll. Jordan, of course, was unfamiliar with the names. Was it Sipho or Simephewi who made 1,600 rand? Or did one of them make 2,000 rand? (Turned out that they were the same person.) He'd make mistakes, and then, as Jordan remembers it, I'd call and chew him out: "People aren't eating today because of you!"

Most of the time, Jordan was almost totally isolated from the South Africa office. We had one dial-up line in Port Elizabeth, so we'd typically send a single e-mail with everything we needed Jordan to know. The phone line was terrible, and that combined with the time difference meant that we mostly communicated by fax. This was not only confusing and frustrating for Jordan, but also meant he was completely divorced from the work we did, the children and families we were helping, all of which kept most of us going.

It was an unfair position, but it was also a crucible: He had to come through it or leave, and after he did come through it, he was an Ubuntu lifer. He'd worked himself raw, but he'd proved that he could manage the entire US operation of a start-up nonprofit—plus, he'd finally learned Excel. He had the pride of having figured this place out and the resolve that came from having devoted himself completely to the organization. Ubuntu was now his passion, too.

After three months of traveling in Southeast Asia, Lindsay and I touched down in Port Elizabeth in early 2002 to stay for four months. I had expected Banks to pick us up at the airport and bring us back to his place to stay. Instead, Gcobani was there. Remember, I'd only met him once at this point, and it had been late in the evening at a *braai*, after having a few beers. It's amazing that I even recognized him.

"Banks sent me to get you," Gcobani said. "And I'm taking you to my home."

We drove to a quiet suburb, to a modest home with a pretty yard and a small pool in the back. I got more and more irritated with Banks with every moment. I didn't want to be in the suburbs—I wanted to be in the townships.

At the same time, here was Gcobani, opening his home for months to a guy he'd met once. He and his wife had three young sons, and hosting two Americans was no small undertaking. But both Gcobani and his wife, Nomsa, handled the situation with grace. Gcobani would talk about his father's generosity as a model for his own. Gcobani had grown up on a farm in the Karoo, where his father worked as a laborer. He couldn't remember a time when there weren't people staying in their house. When his father received wages, he'd often go buy a live goat to slaughter so they'd have meat for a month. But once he slaughtered the goat, he'd give a piece to this neighbor, some to his siblings, to a friend down the road, until there was almost nothing left.

As I got to know Gcobani, I was impressed by his quiet strength, the generosity and kindness that he showed to every person he met, and an openness of spirit that belied the difficult circumstances of his life under apartheid. Although the closest school had been twelve kilometers away, Gcobani and his siblings would walk there every day; his father insisted that education was the only way they'd be liberated. Gcobani would watch the way his father was treated—he describes it as "subhuman"—and his determination to get out hardened.

In the Karoo, children didn't study past grade seven; instead, they'd go back to work on the farm. So Gcobani, at thirteen, was sent to the Transkei, a rural homeland for the Xhosa, to further his education. There, he was around political activists, men and women who had been imprisoned on Robben Island and then sent back to the homeland as a way to isolate them. As Gcobani advanced in school, he grew more and more politically aware as well. At sixteen, now in the New Brighton township of Port Elizabeth, he joined a march protesting apartheid. As the protestors gathered in a square, a huge armored car called a Casspir, which was used widely in putting down protests during apartheid, came toward the square. As people began to run, the soldiers inside opened fire. Gcobani saw others around him falling, and blood spilling onto the pavement. Gcobani leapt the wall of a house and found an outdoor toilet, where he hid until the shooting stopped.

Later, Gcobani and Nomsa, who had met as teenagers, married; the day after their wedding, Gcobani left for England, where he'd received a scholarship to study at Leeds University. They were apart for a year, during which their first son was born. When he came back, he threw himself into teaching, into finding ways to enrich his students' lives both in and out of the classroom.

From my time living in the townships, I knew that everyone had one story from apartheid that had changed everything. One clear night, Gcobani and I sat in his backyard under blazingly bright stars. We started talking about the past, how it felt to grow up under such dehumanizing conditions. And then he told me his story.

~~~~~~

"In 1985, I had a brother-in-law, Sicelo Mhlauli, who was a headmaster in Oudtshoorn," Gcobani began. "He originally was from Cradock. My sister was in Port Elizabeth writing exams, and she was waiting for her husband to come. He was supposed to come on a Thursday; he never pitched up on the Thursday. Later on, we heard

And it wasn't just the mental stress. It was the physical toll the work took, in ways expected and not. We all drank too much, as a way of coping with the stress and the terrible circumstances we were dealing with, day in and out. Over time, I developed an ulcer. It took me by surprise because nobody ever talks about how difficult and complex working in poverty can be. Our culture has made it heroic and over-glamorized it, and people think of it as a romantic lifestyle. But, in reality, we spent every day working in life-threatening situations and witnessing firsthand the realities of poverty: Children suffering malnutrition and abuse. It's one thing to read about these issues and want to help, but another to come face-to-face with a seven-year-old girl who has been raped.

One day, I was the last person left at our office at Emfundweni; all the school's teachers and administrators had gone home, too. A group of kids were playing outside in a lot that served as a dump for the neighborhood. Suddenly, I heard screaming and ran outside. All the kids were huddled around a little boy whose arm was dangling; he had fallen onto a huge piece of jagged glass, and blood was everywhere. I grabbed him, wrapped him up in a blanket, and drove him to the hospital. Only hours later, after he'd been taken care of and the doctors said he'd be okay, did I think about the fact that so many people in the township were HIV-positive, and I'd had blood all over me. Luckily, the test I took soon after—the second HIV test in my life—came back negative, but it was a sobering reminder of the fear our community lived with constantly.

The dangers were ever-present for our staff, too. By this time, we had health educators and educational outreach workers who would go out in the community to run workshops and provide services. Most of our staff came from the township and still lived there, and we didn't have the resources to provide any kind of security when they were out in the community. In 2001, when I was still in the United States, one of our health workers, a woman named Thandi, had been out late and was walking home. Four men attacked her; all four raped her, and then they sliced her open with a knife, leaving her bleeding in the bush. Amazingly, she survived the night. A passerby the next morning heard her moans and took her to the hospital.

We didn't have health insurance for our workers and we didn't know what to do. I was half a world away, and twenty-four years old, and had no idea how to cope with this kind of trauma. Banks would visit her and bring her soup and bread, but we didn't have any response in place: no funds, no counseling, no kind of medical leave with pay we could give her. We did what we could, and what we thought was right, but we knew it wasn't enough. She recovered as well as she could, but she never came back to work with us. I still see her from time to time, and though she always smiles and greets me happily, I see the change in her eyes and I know that we let her down.

Her case was particularly brutal, but every day someone faced some kind of danger or instability. From the beginning, we'd set out to hire from the community. In some cases, we'd meet someone who needed help and all we had to offer was a job, and so that's what we gave them. But as we began to grow as an organization, I knew we needed to offer more than a salary; we needed to take care of our employees, too.

~~~~~~~

In late 2001 and into 2002, we started to hire more staff for our school resource centers, and we were developing our plans to begin building school libraries: the Siyafunda ("We Are Reading") Library Initiative. I was in the office interviewing people for a computer resource job and soon met a charismatic young man named Qondakele Sompondo. As he was waiting, he looked over some of our materials about our current and upcoming programs, and he told me, "I'd really like to apply for this library job." His degree was in library science, and he felt passionate about the idea of bringing books into the schools—something that had never been done before in the townships. I told him that job didn't exist, and that the library program wasn't going to get started for another six months. "I'll wait," he said.

I was won over. We brought him on, and over the next few years, he helped us build eight school libraries. Qondakele was from the townships, and he felt driven to make a change for the children who lived there. "I was born in the community, and went to school here, with broken windows, no tables, no chairs," he told me. He'd graduated in 1993, but even now, the school was the same. "It took me fifteen years to shake off the bad education I got. That's what's killing South Africa," he said. "You can't really change the system. But you can take a small group and change that."

～～～～～

The complexity of life in the township continuously came home to me, especially during the four months Lindsay and I spent living with Gcobani. It was the longest stretch I'd been in South Africa since I'd lived with Banks in the railway flats, and being with the community again helped me think more deeply about the mission of Ubuntu. Banks and I were both committed to listening and responding to needs, even if it meant evolving dramatically as an organization.

One day, Gcobani asked me if I'd like to come by his poetry club and help out. He'd started the program as an after-school activity, with ten eleven-year-olds in a room together, writing and reading their poetry. Writing poetry allowed them to express their feelings, their anxiety and their fear, their sadness and their joy. It became an escape for me, in some ways, to go and spend this time with kids, instead of thinking about donors, about strategy, about budgets.

Quite naturally, writing poetry would lead to homework help. So we'd stay for an extra hour to go over math or biology or history. Gradually, we started to do more: take students to doctor's appointments, bring them food to eat, and drive them home. Seeing where and how the children lived felt like a slap in the face; suddenly, all the work we did seemed totally inadequate. One evening, Lwando, a skinny young boy who could do a killer Mandela impression, asked if we could take him home—we'd stayed so late that it was dark, and he had to go across a major road to get to his house. We got in my car and he gave me directions, and we pulled up to a tiny shack made of corrugated zinc. I walked him inside, and realized he was living there alone. The door stood ajar behind us, because it didn't fit properly in the frame. Through the darkness, I could see a thin mattress in one corner. The room was damp and penetratingly cold.

I learned later that his mother had abandoned Lwando as a baby. His paternal grandmother took him in, though her son never acknowledged Lwando as his own. When Lwando's grandmother passed away, he didn't know any other family members who were willing to care for him, so he stayed there alone, barely surviving. I thought about our computer centers, about the libraries we were beginning to build, even our health initiative, and it didn't seem like enough. Over these four months with the poetry club, I slowly became aware that we needed to aim to do more. Unlike with our health initiative, this wasn't a thunderbolt moment, and nothing happened right away—it would take years of figuring out how to effectively change how Ubuntu worked. But it was clear that the only way you could invest in a child was to start with a stable home. The most fundamental change for Ubuntu happened more like a river carving a new bank: each day, the force of the work we were doing pressed us along, and slowly we began to forge a more direct path toward our goals.

~~~~~~

We didn't have the funds to immediately launch all the initiatives we wanted to put in place, and we'd made commitments to, and still believed in, projects like computer labs and libraries. And community buy-in remained at the root of everything that we did. We discussed every new plan and every substantial modification of an existing plan with principals and teachers and parents, going through round after round of exhaustive and sometimes exhausting meetings.

At times, I'd get frustrated and say to Banks, "I know exactly what these teachers are going to say. Let's skip this meeting and start doing something."

Banks, the consummate community builder, would laugh at my impatience. "Jake, the process matters. Even if you know the outcome, we need to have the meeting."

As with any working relationship, sometimes tension built between Ubuntu and the community, particularly as we tried to work with the principal and teachers at Emfundweni while Banks continued to teach and we both worked on Ubuntu out of our little office there. The teachers didn't seem committed to working in the computer center, and I had grown frustrated with the dull incompetence that seemed to characterize so many of our interactions with the school personnel. I often had a difficult time biting my tongue when someone appeared to be acting inappropriately, or undermined our work in some way. Banks would step in to calm me down. He knew how to absorb blows without striking back, to wait until emotions had cooled and it was possible to have a reasonable discussion.

The nadir of our relationship with the school came in 2002, when we opened the Irving Lief Siyafunda Library, a small, sturdy building set in the back courtyard of Emfundweni. A student had painted the entire building with a mural depicting scenes of learning and storytelling, and the bright exterior reflected the energy and hope that had gone into its construction. We'd named it after my grandfather, a tough-as-nails Bostonian who definitely believed in the school of hard knocks. He was the kind of guy's guy who believed in watching baseball and enjoying a good whiskey, and I'm not sure he ever understood my desire to go to Africa. While I was living with Banks in the railroad flats that first summer, he'd died. I didn't have a cell phone or a reliable means of communicating with my family, so I didn't know about it until after the burial. Banks was with me when I heard the news, and he told me solemnly, "Jake, we must honor the ancestors. We must do something for him." And so, four years later, we named this library for the students of Emfundweni after him.

Given its connection to my grandfather, this library, our first, had particular emotional weight for me. Lindsay and my parents traveled to Port Elizabeth for the opening, and the days were filled with nervous anticipation. The first sign of trouble came in a shipping container full of books. A few months before the library opened, *National Geographic* had written a short piece about Ubuntu, and a high school student in Seattle had read it and decided to organize a book drive for Emfundweni's library. She worked very hard to gather as many books as possible so that we could fill the shelves, but she clearly hadn't realized that she could—and should—reject some of the donations. When the shipping container arrived, it contained twenty-five copies of a PhD dissertation on agriculture in Western Australia, encyclopedias so outdated they identified a region of Africa as the Belgian Congo, and coloring books that had already been filled in. Imagine how devastated you'd be as a child to open up a coloring book and find that it was all done!

Yet people at Emfundweni were so thrilled that a shipping container of books had been sent to them, they didn't care. They put all these books in the library, and thought it was wonderful. I wasn't happy about it—I didn't think that these books were worthy. Donating a book or clothing isn't charitable if it's something you'd otherwise throw away. It should be an investment, of the same quality you'd buy for yourself. I took the principal aside and asked him, "How can you put books like this out for the children? They aren't useful, they aren't in good shape. The students deserve better."

The answer he gave devastated me. He looked at me and said coolly, "Beggars can't be choosers."

The opening ceremony arrived a few days later. I stood in the courtyard under a beautiful blue sky with Lindsay and my parents. Ubuntu had set up a tent and a marquee; it was a big day for us, and we wanted to celebrate. After everyone spoke a few words, my father and I cut the ribbon, and we all stepped inside for the first time, along with Banks. And there, covering an entire wall, was a huge banner thanking the girl who had sent the books. Ubuntu had put hundreds of hours into this library, trying to provide a quality resource. Yet the school deliberately chose to celebrate a donation that was subpar.

I realized that this was the way that the school had decided to put us in our place, and I was angry. I turned to Banks and said, "We're leaving Emfundweni Primary School for good, today. We can't work with them anymore."

Banks grabbed my arm and said quickly, "Jake, I understand. But let's talk about it tomorrow."

I calmed down, and we stayed there for another year before moving to a larger office. But my heart and soul left that day. That moment made me sad and angry in equal measures: sad that so many in the community truly believed they deserved no better than already filled-in coloring books and out-of-date encyclopedias, and angry that a man in the position to change that attitude sought only to reinforce it.

With my original group of Ndzondelelo Secondary School students (1998)

Visiting some of the boys from the railway flats in the "bush" during their circumcision ritual (1998)

Another night, another party in the railway flats (1998)

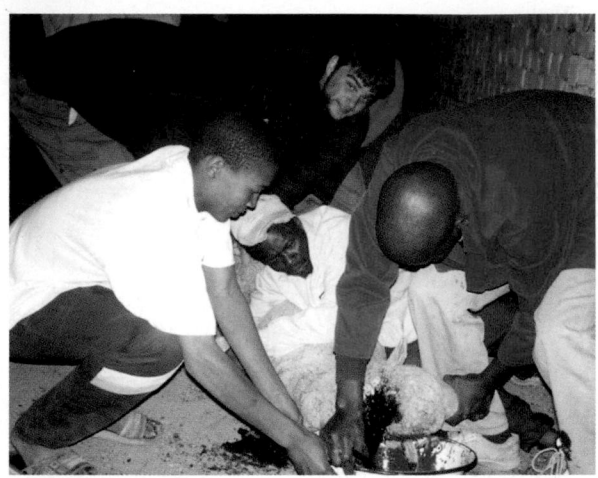

Helping to slaughter a sheep with Daniel Friedland for Pumi's son's return from the bush (1998)

Banks, me, Micky, Mlingani, and Sloo a few weeks after I moved in (1998)

Hanging *loxion*-style (1998)

With Rasta Chris at the railway flats —biggest Kaizer Chiefs fan I know (1999)

Banks handing over our first delivery of school supplies (1999)

Banks and me canvassing the townships (2000, James Baigrie)

With my parents and Lindsay on a seven-day camping trip in the Okavango Delta (2000)

Banks with some of our students in the first Ubuntu Computer Lab (2001, Karen Stead Baigrie)

Kids playing football in the streets of Zwide (2001, Karen Stead Baigrie)

Lindsay and me
at the opening of
the Irving Lief
Siyafunda Library
(2002)

Family portrait with me, Abongile, Nomsa, Phelelani, and Gcobani (2002)

A *braai* from the early years (2003)

Leading the Young Ambassadors on a five-day trail in Baviaanskloof Nature Reserve (2003)

Some of our clients in New Brighton township (2003, Karen Stead Baigrie)

Jana leading a buy-in workshop in Kwazakhele (2004)

My brother Matthew days after arriving in Port Elizabeth (2005)

Banks, me, and Archbishop Tutu before our first-ever gala (2006)

President Clinton and Zethu in New York City (2007, Clinton Global Initiative)

Floating down the river in Kafue, Zambia, with my brother Matthew, our then board chairman Daniel Osorio, and my friend Adam Ring (2007, Sung Hee Choe)

Lindsay and me the night before our wedding (2007)

After our first-ever London gala with (*clockwise*) Hugh Masekela, me, Gcobani, Lara Tabatznik, and Zethu Ngceza (2008)

I don't usually wear a tie but I don't usually visit 10 Downing Street (2008)

Lungi speaking at our tenth anniversary gala (2009, Ben Hider)

Backstage with Dave Matthews and Vusi Mahlasela at our NYC gala (2010)

The Ubuntu Centre (2010, Aris Vrakas)

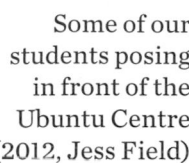

Building a business with friends is tough but has its perks—World Cup fever with Jordan and Jana (2010)

Some of our students posing in front of the Ubuntu Centre (2012, Jess Field)

Felix, Nozi, Lwando, and Siya—all university graduates today (2011)

Zwide township (2012, Aris Vrakas)

Zethu on graduation day (2012, Ongama Mtimka)

There is nothing more sustainable than investing in a child every day of their lives (2012, Tim Hans)

Jana, Jordan, Tarryn, Ziyanda Ntshona (Ubuntu board member), Kim Howard (Ubuntu board member), Gcobani, and Banks with President Clinton and Chelsea Clinton at the Ubuntu Centre (2013, Riann Labuschangne)

Your birthplace should not determine your future. Lithemba, age three, standing outside his home dressed up as his dream profession of a doctor (2012, Tim Hans)

Inaugural class of children graduating from our early childhood development program (2013, Tim Hans)

With Michael Franti, a longtime Ubuntu friend (2014)

CHANGING THE CONVERSATION: MEASURING IMPACT

BIGGER, FASTER, CHEAPER. This mentality has infected the nonprofit sector as organizations react to the rise of impact investing, prevalence of charity-rating agencies, and heightened focus on scale. Development workers fixate on how to reach x amount of people in y regions over the course of z months, because funding, legitimacy, and recognition primarily stem from generating big numbers. Dependent on a fixed grant cycle, organizations abandon long-term, slow-growth investments in favor of short-term, number-intensive interventions—privileging outputs over outcomes. Suddenly, distributing a million windup computers, despite having no idea or even concern over whether the recipients will be able to use them effectively, trumps producing a hundred university graduates.

It's an issue, in many ways, of comparing apples to oranges. The sliding scale used by charity-rating agencies flattens out the varied landscape of the development world. Handing out computers can be a valuable intervention in its own way. Giving a child a bed net has a profound impact: It saves lives by reducing the risk of contracting malaria. But that impact is not the same as the impact of providing household stability, health, and educational support to a child for more than a decade. These valuable interventions have wildly divergent costs in both time and money. Yet they are too often judged in the same way by foundations and donors.

Focusing on outputs and employing a narrow definition of scale oversimplifies the complexity of poverty. Distributing a thousand cups of soup will help hungry children, but this strategy will never fully address a household's pervasive food insecurity. We have to realize that raising children and helping families access upward socioeconomic mobility isn't scalable in the same way that building schools or handing out drinking straw water filters is. And it cannot be done in a twelve-month grant cycle.

—

Ashish J. Thakkar is an entrepreneur based in United Arab Emirates and Uganda who founded the Mara Group, a multisector investment group, and Mara Foundation, which provides support for young entrepreneurs in

(continued)

Africa. He started his first business at the age of fifteen with a $5,000 loan; most recently, he launched Atlas Mara Co-Nvest, a financial services group, with Bob Diamond, the former chief executive of Barclays. "The fact that only 9 percent of people have access to real banking services yet we have 80 percent mobile phone penetration on the continent is hugely significant," Thakkar explained to me recently. "This shows you that this is a sector that needs to be 'disrupted.'"

The mentality of "bigger, cheaper, faster" seems like it could become more and more problematic for the social sector, particularly in terms of its potential impact on our longer-term priorities. To be on the main stage at the World Economic Forum in Davos or Clinton Global Initiative, you have to boast that you are working with a hundred thousand people or are in thirty regions. This then creates a culture where local organizations are not able to look at long-term priorities, but instead focus on short-term wins that may look "big," but don't have a sustainable impact. What if you were to take fifty entrepreneurs and ensure that they are winners as opposed to a hundred thousand?

THAKKAR: There is no right or wrong in this. I think "bigger and faster" should absolutely be associated with the social sector. With regard to "cheaper," I think people need to think about what can be done in the most cost-effective and self-sustaining manner. We have a lot of impact to create and we must create it now. We must think big and do things in a more extreme manner. We have a billion people on the continent, and I am very passionate about touching as many lives as possible. Our program Mara Mentor is currently impacting over one hundred thousand entrepreneurs, and we are growing this number every day. But organizations like Endeavor Global, for example, work with a handful of entrepreneurs and really are taking them to the next level.

Now, is the Mara Mentor model wrong? No, it's hitting masses and really touching lives. Is the Endeavor Global model wrong in that they are only working with a few organizations? Absolutely not—they are really scaling these organizations up and making a difference. There is room and necessity for both models. My personal passion is that I want to be able to move the needle [for these billion people on the continent] when it comes to entrepreneurship and truly enable and inspire young male and female entrepreneurs.

I would challenge someone with your skills, your ability, and your experience to think about inculcating your knowledge and skill set into a hundred people instead of a hundred thousand. Could you have a larger impact?

THAKKAR: Probably. The challenge again is to decide what you are most passionate about. This is where social enterprises, philanthropy, nonprofits—call it what you will—play a vital role. The bottom line is that no matter what title you give it, it's what you want to make a difference in. What you've done at Ubuntu is unbelievable—you have taken these two thousand kids to a new level. You are enabling them to get a job that they have never dreamed of and that their peers have never dreamed of. That is your passion and you want to truly impact these two thousand lives. My passion is that I want to truly impact millions of entrepreneurs across the continent; if some of them can really take advantage of these opportunities and go to the next level, that's fantastic. If others can inspire more people to make a difference, then that's also excellent. I really want to tap into the youth of the continent, and that's what I'm most passionate about.

What's the value you see in local knowledge and the value of context when investing? What's the importance of this local knowledge?

THAKKAR: In Africa, we have forty-six sub-Saharan countries. Each country is so unique and independent we all have our own cultures, histories, parliaments, and politics. How do you operate in a truly local manner with global standards? How do you make that happen? This is the big opportunity that I see on the continent. Mara's Theme, which is exactly the same as Atlas Mara's, is combining the best of global and local. In Atlas Mara's case, it is taking Bob's global knowledge and merging it with Mara's local experience. We then want to combine the best of entrepreneurial and institutional knowledge—operating in an institutional manner with the right governing structures, but still very entrepreneurial and having an ability to do things that other people can't do. This blend, which resonates with Mara and with Atlas Mara, really ascribes to our philosophy of "do good and do well."

When thinking about an investment, how do you assess whether a really great idea might be handicapped by political or social factors?

THAKKAR: I think it really depends on what you are trying to do and how you are trying to achieve it. If you are playing in sectors that are sensitive to

(continued)

governments, such as natural resources or extractive industries, I think it's most dangerous. Extractive industries can be very messy. Therefore, Mara has a policy that it doesn't invest in extractive industries—we just don't want to get involved in things that can potentially have those issues. I don't like things that are too dependent on government. The most important thing is that if you are going to take part in activities that are driven around too much government influence, licenses, or incentives, it's always going to be controversial. If you are doing things that just complement or make a difference, it's not an issue.

So how would you advise global investors to get involved with Africa?

THAKKAR: I would say that it needs to be in the manner where it is truly impactful. It needs to be in line with their passion and what an organization is most excited about. Everybody has his or her own focus areas. Backing organizations and individuals that have the ability to execute and are willing to put real passion behind what they are trying to achieve is the way to go. This type of investing must be done in a practical way and for the right reasons. You must give freedom to the people who are conducting these exercises. It's very theoretical to think that you can help improve, etc., but the guys doing it on the ground have a lot more know-how. You must trust them enough to empower them with the skills they need to achieve their goals.

CHAPTER SIX

Outputs
vs.
Outcomes

I MET JORDAN AND HIS GIRLFRIEND, JANA ZINDELL, IN THE DEPARTURES area at JFK. "Okay, guys, here's a notebook with some common Xhosa phrases you might want to know," I told them while we sat at a bar downing Bloody Marys. "We're going straight to the office from the airport, so try to get some sleep on the plane."

Jordan and Jana looked at each other. I saw the thought *Is this really a good idea?* flash between them.

By the time Lindsay and I had returned to the United States in the spring of 2002, Jordan had been indoctrinated in all things Ubuntu, and he'd brought Jana, who'd been working in PR but was itching to do something else, into the fold as well. He had pushed me to send him to South Africa so he could be a part of the programs, but it hadn't made sense for him or for us at that point. So instead, he had gone to the

London School of Economics to get his master's in development management, and Jana had done the same at Georgetown University.

The pair reunited in Wisconsin a year later to finish up their theses. Jordan called me one afternoon. "Jake, we're ready. Jana and I want to work in development, and we both want to work at Ubuntu, in Port Elizabeth. Do you have anything available?"

At the time, we were still struggling to find our leadership team in South Africa. Early on, my cousin, Eric Cooper, and his friends Paul Newell and Adam Schwartz had come down to help us because we had no money to hire anyone. They stayed for a year, and then Adam and Eric moved on. Paul, who reminded me of Gcobani in his relentless kindness and energy for Ubuntu, returned to New York and began running our US office; he stayed with us for nine years. But their departure from Port Elizabeth left a vacuum there, and to have people join us whom I trusted implicitly, and who had fresh academic experience in development, felt like the perfect solution. He and Jana had completed our usual hiring process, of course, even if it wasn't very arduous, and one day we met outside the New York Public Library to sign their new contracts. I gave them my version of an orientation. "You don't need a car, I can drive you guys. No one at the office eats lunch, and it will make people uncomfortable if you guys bring something in."

Looking back on it now, I'm amazed they endured those first months working for us. Jordan and Jana took my words to heart. They'd work all day, with little to eat for twelve, thirteen hours. I'd set up their jobs so that Jana worked in the morning and early afternoon, while Jordan worked later in the day with the development committee, which met when Banks and Gcobani left their schools in the afternoon. Thoughtlessly, I'd basically engineered it so they would never see each other outside of work. And, while it was true that when I was in South Africa I could drive them, I wasn't in South Africa the entire time they were.

Finally fed up, Jordan started scouring the classifieds for a used car. At a disadvantage because he didn't drive a manual transmission, he finally found a listing for an automatic: a 1980 Toyota Corolla. Banks, Jordan, Jana, and I all crammed into my tiny car to go look at it. From the backseat, Jana asked skeptically, "What are you even going to do when we get there? None of you guys know anything about cars."

"Don't worry, we've got this under control," Banks and I reassured her. We met the owner in the parking lot of a KFC. He was a big guy with an Afrikaner accent wearing khaki short shorts and long socks. He didn't look happy to see Banks with us. Without even greeting us, he said, "Do you want the car or not?" Jordan told him we wanted to check it out first. Jana decided not to get involved, but the rest of us walked around the car. Banks opened up the hood and started fiddling around inside, though he had no idea what he was looking at. I actually kicked the tires.

By this point, the guy was clearly starting to get angry. Jordan said, "Okay, look, let us take it for a test drive." The owner wouldn't allow us take it alone, so we all piled in, with the owner at the wheel, and drove around the block. The car stalled four times. When we got back to the parking lot, Jordan pulled Banks and I aside and asked, "I don't know, guys. Should I take it?" Banks and I both paused to think it over.

"Yeah, I think you should take it," I said, and Banks nodded along.

Jordan handed over his life savings for the car. Three months later, the car was dead. Sometimes Jordan and Jana laughed about their bad luck; other times it was hard not to see it as a bad omen.

Despite the lack of training, despite the insane demands of their jobs, despite leaving the office each day feeling like they had no more to give, Jordan and Jana stuck with it. Jana's survival through this period is the most stunning. She came to the office to work on an initiative to make our computer centers profitable, which turned out to be an impossible task. The demand wasn't there, and it didn't make sense to push it. But for several months, Jana was tasked with trying to get people trained, to drum up interest, to press forward despite obstacles. She's a strong, forthright woman who isn't afraid to speak her mind, and she's driven; she could see possibility here, the challenge thrilled her, and she had passion for the work. But she was a white American woman in a position in which women, especially younger women, traditionally deferred to men.

People started to whisper that she was too pushy, that she was only here because she was Jordan's girlfriend. No matter what she suggested, it was immediately treated with suspicion. Most hurtfully, some charged that she didn't respect their culture. Culture carries a sacred connotation, and for a long time, I saw respecting culture as the most important aspect of working in our community. But then I saw culture being used as a way to defend things like rape and abuse, and I realized that culture can and should evolve: Think about all the words and actions that were once deemed culturally appropriate in the United States. There's no reason that culture should trump basic human rights.

Meanwhile, Jordan's role as strategic advisor, helping to shape our senior leadership meetings into something more along the lines of a business model, was swiftly evolving into a more substantial one. When he and Jana had moved to Port Elizabeth, Ubuntu had still been caught up in the start-up phase, unable to take the next step. Banks and I both have strong personalities, a ton of passion, and a clear dedication to this project, and Ubuntu would never have gotten off the ground if we weren't both totally unattached to the way things are normally done. Gcobani, who by this time was part of our senior leadership team, was serious and intellectual, but he'd never run a business. We needed someone to come in and say, "Hey, let's take this step by step. First we brainstorm, then we do feasibility studies, then we figure out a budget. When it gets going, let's keep monitoring the effectiveness of these programs, and make sure they're working for us." Jordan brought in another perspective that helped get our discussions moving along when we started to stagnate in old debates.

I argued a lot with both Jana and Jordan during this time. My mindset was "There's the goal. Let's sprint as fast as we can, as hard as we can, as long as we can, and get there." That took us far for a long time, because in the beginning we had to have that drive. But I didn't think a lot about a more holistic way of doing business, one where we take care of employees as well as clients so that people work better and want to stay with the organization. I thought and talked a lot about sustainability in our programming, but I'd never recognized that we needed to sustain our staff, too. Both Jordan and Jana saw that we needed to make a transition from a collection of people fueled by enthusiasm to a real professional organization if we wanted to be more effective in the community and accomplish the big goals we had in mind.

They were right, and we got there, with plenty of heated debate along the way. But we had a long history and a lot of trust between us, and we could fight and get angry without losing sight of our friendship. We all cared about each other and about Ubuntu, and this made it possible for us to work through all these transitions together.

~~~~~~~

Of course, we played as hard as we worked. We were all in our midtwenties and working seventy- or eighty-hour weeks, and we had to blow off steam somehow. One weekend soon after Jordan and Jana arrived, I took them to the Transkei. We started at the coast, where white beaches nestle between verdant cliffs that plunge into the waves of the Indian Ocean. A few hundred feet from the water sit clusters of huts, where you can buy oysters, mussels, crayfish, and lobsters. We bought a dozen lobsters for about thirty cents each—Xhosa fisherman use them as bait, so they tend to be cheap—and had a feast.

As we made our way inland the next afternoon, the landscape turned to rolling hills and then mountains, and the road often ran next to clear, rapid rivers. As dusk fell, we arrived at a small village along a river. In one of the *rondavels* (round, thatched-roof huts), a *sangoma* ritual was in progress, and we were invited in to take part. Inside, a huge pile of marijuana reached toward the ceiling. It'd been lit underneath, and smoke filled the *rondavel*. Propulsive drums provided a rhythm for the *sangoma* to enter a trance state. We spent hours in that hut dancing, high from the smoke; the heat from the fire and crowd left us all drenched in sweat. When we finally made our way out, we ran into the river. There was a full moon, and we stood there, letting the water and the night air wash away the fevered ritual. As we climbed up the bank, I fell hard on my side, but, still fogged with smoke, I shook it off.

The next day, driving back to Port Elizabeth, we were in terrible shape. We had to stop the car frequently so we all could get violently sick, and I could barely move from pain, though I'd completely forgotten about falling. By the time we limped into Port Elizabeth, Jana was dehydrated and weak and suffering from tick-bite fever. Jordan was depleted as well, and with every step, it felt like a dagger was digging into my side. When Banks saw me, he insisted on taking me to New Brighton to see his doctor, who saw patients in the back room of a tiny house. She took in my symptoms, listened to my lungs, and then solemnly told me, "You have cancer."

Numb from shock, I listened to her instructions about getting follow-up x-rays the next day to determine the cancer's spread. Banks, tears streaming down his face, embraced me. Over the next twenty-four hours, I grappled with the news. I called Lindsay, who was back in Philadelphia at medical school, but decided to wait to tell my parents. I took Jordan to the beach and tearfully told him that I might be dying.

The next day, I went to the hospital for x-rays. I sat nervously in the exam room, waiting to hear my prognosis. The doctor came in and asked, "Did you fall recently?" I immediately said no, but then something tugged at the back of my mind. "Wait," I said. "I did fall, a couple of days ago."

The doctor smiled. "When you fell, you broke a rib," he said. "You don't have cancer, you have a fracture."

I'm not sure anyone has been happier to hear they've broken a bone. When I saw Banks, I told him that he should stop seeing his doctor in New Brighton, that she'd totally misdiagnosed me. "No, man," he said. "She's very good, I promise."

~~~~~~

Inspired by Gcobani's poetry club, and the obvious need those students had for more support both in and out of the classroom, we started to think about ways to go deeper into each child's life. We saw the transformative impact we had on those eight children, and it made us think about the forty thousand we talked about reaching and what we were actually doing for them. The senior leadership would meet each day after Gcobani and Banks arrived from school, and we'd talk about how to break out of the model of building two computer centers and a library every year. These were good projects, and we'd had success in advocating for the township of Joe Slovo to gain a new school, but it didn't feel like enough. These senior leadership meetings would go on for hours, with everyone having an opinion, a story, and an argument that had to be heard. And we often left late at night without any solutions, and totally spent—emotionally, physically, and intellectually.

Yet we slowly began to shape what we wanted to be, and where we were going. There was no blueprint for getting kids out of poverty, so we had room to be creative and be bold, and we weren't afraid of failure or of making mistakes. And when we did make them, we were brutally honest about it. This willingness to risk and to learn helped us create a culture of innovation and an attitude of questioning even the most deep-seated beliefs of the development world.

Jordan, Jana, Qondakele, Gcobani, Banks, and I realized that relying on numbers had begun to oversimplify and dehumanize the work we were doing. The children we worked with, all of whom had very specific circumstances and needs, were being flattened into statistics. I felt the same way about the word "shack"—it was evocative and gave a listener an instant image of what I was talking about, but it also turned someone's home into a symbol of poverty. Yes, they were built of corrugated zinc, they weren't secure or heated or equipped with running water, for the most part. But the people who lived there took meticulous care of their homes, decorated them with wallpaper and knickknacks, and made them as comfortable as possible. Calling a home like this a "shack"—even though no other adequate word existed—felt like I was stripping its occupants of their dignity and their humanity.

We kept coming back to the idea of replication—what people in the development world were beginning to call "scale." In order for people in the outside world to see you as successful, you had to reach enormous numbers of people across enormous areas of the world. We were catering to this with our emphasis on the forty thousand children we reached. It was true, but we only touched them. Eradicating "technological apartheid" and distributing a million condoms were both great things, but they were outputs; they didn't make a child's day-to-day life easier or significantly alter the course of her life. We wanted to embrace these children, even if it meant that we changed two thousand lives rather than touching forty thousand.

～～～～

Over the years, we'd often returned to a few basic beliefs that guided Ubuntu. The six of us started to call them our pillars: They were what formed the foundation for our work. Primary among these was a geographical boundary for Ubuntu, a seven-kilometer area with a community of about 400,000 people. We wanted to be able to stay focused, and this was the place we knew and that knew us. Beginning to work in another township somewhere else in South Africa would have meant learning a whole new approach to our work and investing months, probably years, of building community trust and buy-in before we could implement one program.

In the same vein, hiring from within the community became even more important to our success as an organization. We needed to hire people who could engage respectfully with parents, who knew how to get a mother to come in for HIV testing or to get on medication, to come in for counseling or workshops in parenting. Once you go into a child's home, after all, you start getting into some dark places. Whether it's a functional home or a dysfunctional home, you're in someone's private life.

Slowly, we began to take a different approach to our hiring. In the beginning, we'd sometimes hire someone because they needed a job and they demonstrated a desire to give back. The only thing we'd had to give was a job. This felt consistent with our mission, and with the spirit of *ubuntu* that had inspired us. As we began to look at expanding our services, providing more specialized and more sensitive interventions, it became clear that we needed people who were efficient and professional. We still believed that the best person for the job might not have a formal background in a particular area, but we needed people who showed aptitude, drive, and passion. And we realized that hiring with that mind-set was still consistent with the spirit of *ubuntu*, because we were both serving the community better and providing a better workplace for our staff.

Next, what does it mean to impact a child's life? We always focused on university or employment as the measure of success, but when you're confronted with a seven-year-old girl who has been raped and lives by herself in a shack, there are a lot of steps to take between there and university. In that kind of situation, all the good work that gets done during the day disappears in the night. To make sustained inroads in a child's life, we need to stabilize her home environment.

I went to a meeting once with a guy who could not understand what we did and why we were working in children's homes. I asked him, "Do you have children?" He pointed to the photos on his desk. "Three, all in college."

"How did they get there?" I asked. "They didn't get there from going to school in a shipping container with a teacher who doesn't have a high school degree. They got there because of the amount of love and attention and, frankly, money you put into them. If they needed help in a subject, you got them tutoring. If they couldn't see the blackboard, you got them glasses. If they were sick, you took them to a doctor; if they needed a dentist, they saw one." All parents want to get their children successfully from birth to adulthood. So they provide a secure home and enough food, support, and guidance. And they give each of their children different things, because every child has different challenges: One has a peanut allergy, the other one doesn't. One is dyslexic, the other one has trouble with math. When you raise children, you give them, as best you can, whatever they need—from health care to clothing to a feeling of security—in order to thrive.

So why did people think you could do anything less in the townships and still expect real change? Yes, we could put computers in a school, and that was great. But the child who now knew how to work on a computer was going home to an HIV-positive mother, was living in a house with poor ventilation and security, and didn't have regular meals. So how was learning word processing helping this child? We needed to start focusing on outcomes: Did our work help change the course of a child's life? If a child goes home to no food, to physical or emotional abuse, to no electricity and holes in the ceiling so that during the rainy season they're kept up all night shivering in puddles, no amount of math and science tutoring is going to make a significant difference.

~~~~~~

Perhaps the most difficult work we needed to take on was sexual abuse. Nearly 60 percent of the girls Ubuntu works with in the township have been raped by the time they turn eighteen, whether by a parent, an uncle, a neighbor, or a stranger—or, sometimes, a peer. Children who suffer abuse can go on to abuse other children. One day at Emfundweni, one of our health educators told me that she'd walked into a kindergarten classroom and found five girls sitting on the floor, penetrating each other with rolled up pieces of paper. This is not typical behavior for a five-year-old. The teacher asked for our help. We discovered that the same neighbor had abused all five girls.

And, sadly, this wasn't incredibly unusual. At times, it seemed as though every child we worked with had been abused. In response, we trained our health workers to provide counseling for rape and abuse victims. We had a lot of models to draw from, and as we thought about working with girls on empowerment and self-esteem, we had plenty of examples to emulate there, too. But it seemed obvious to us that in focusing only on girls, we would be missing an important half of the equation. We set out to create gender relations workshops aimed at boys and men to take the burden of preventing abuse off women.

We were working, slowly, toward a more comprehensive approach to our work. What were the steps we had to follow to get a child out of poverty? Make sure the house they lived in was a safe, stable place. Help all the members of the family stay as healthy as possible. Give the student the educational tools to succeed in school. These were the fundamental services we had to be prepared to provide. Of course, there was plenty more to do, but as with any kind of parenting, we had to always be ready to evolve, to respond to needs as they arose, and to constantly assess and reassess what we were doing.

~~~~~~

Around this time, I began attending development conferences all over the world. It was a way to raise our profile—just being there signals that you are important enough, savvy enough, to be taken seriously—but I also hoped that we could find new ideas and new strategies through the many discussions and presentations. I met a lot of thought-provoking, dedicated, high-powered people at these conferences. One year, at a World Economic Forum regional conference in Cape Town, I attended a panel discussion that included William Easterly, the New

York University economist. His frank assessments of some of the big players in the development world—including, famously, his skepticism of the large-scale interventions promoted by Jeffrey Sachs, the economist who acts as a special advisor to the United Nations on its Millennium Development Goals—thrilled me. This guy was speaking my language. He neatly defined two broad camps in the development world, one of which I'd noticed in my own work. As he writes in his excellent book *The White Man's Burden*:

> *In foreign aid, Planners announce good intentions but don't motivate anyone to carry them out; Searchers find things that work and get some reward. Planners raise expectations but take no responsibility for meeting them; Searchers accept responsibility for their actions. Planners determine what to supply; Searchers find out what is in demand. Planners apply global blueprints; Searchers adapt to local conditions. Planners at the top lack knowledge of the bottom; Searchers find out what the reality is at the bottom. Planners never hear whether the planned got what it needed; Searchers find out if the customer is satisfied.*

And, he adds, "The right plan is to have no plan": In many ways, that could be Ubuntu's motto.

Still, much of the time I left these conferences thinking, *What is being accomplished here?* The focus often seems to be on pure numbers—how many people you reach, how many regions you are in, how low is your overhead—without seriously asking how great an impact these programs have on an individual's life. I saw a lot of organizations caught up in their own cycle of trying to reach more people, to tout higher numbers, to impress more donors, to get more money—forgetting that all these numbers represent real people, with real problems. And I became frustrated by the obsession with finding a silver-bullet solution when it was so clear to me that what works is age-old, commonsense, and simple.

I started being invited to sit on panels. (Another, perhaps necessary, issue I have with these conferences is that they always place me out front: It feels false to be positioned as the face of Ubuntu. By this time, all the important thinking about our work was being done by a "we," not an "I." Banks, Gcobani, Jordan, Jana, Qondakele, and I needed each other; not one of us would have moved Ubuntu forward in the way that all of us together did.) At one conference on postconflict education, there were nearly a hundred people in the room, including some of the most respected names in philanthropy and education. The moderator opened the discussion by saying, "This action network must come up with innovative solutions to postconflict education. We need to come up with new ways of doing this, because we're not making enough of an inroad." A few other people on the panel spoke, while I quietly fumed.

Finally, I spoke up. "With all due respect, why do we need to come up with 'innovative solutions to postconflict education'?" I asked. "I think that's the whole problem. We attend these conferences regularly and talk about new solutions and no one's going back to basics. We need to think simple, and we need to go back to what works."

I turned to the moderator. "Do you have children?" She nodded. "Do you know how to raise your child?" She frowned slightly and said, "Where are you going with this?"

"It seems like a commonsense principle to me," I said. "The challenge isn't finding innovation. It is finding ways to implement and execute basic childrearing concepts in poor and developing areas."

The audience peppered me with questions, and it seemed that what I had said resonated with some, and offended others. It strikes me as unfortunate that this approach—affording the same dignity to and investing in the same quality for a poor child as you would for your own—is so often received as provocative.

~~~~~~

Maybe it was the sheer cost of our approach. The programs we were developing weren't cheap, and we were willing to invest thousands of dollars in a single child because we saw that that was the most effective strategy. But the annual funding cycles of the development sector have been set up in a way that demands low overhead and a vast scale of people reached, and encourages short-term thinking.

Once, Ubuntu received a one-year grant meant to help a hundred students pass their matric exam, which allowed them to graduate from high school. In our area, on cold winter nights, people often bring their coal into their shacks to help stay warm. One night, someone fell asleep with a coal still burning. These shacks sit only two or three feet from the next, so when one shack is set on fire, they all go up in flames. In a matter of hours, hundreds of people were homeless, including more than half of our students. Would those kids be studying as well as they should at night or making it to school in the morning? No, they didn't have a home anymore—they'd be worried about surviving, not about the exam.

Of the remaining students, another half of them had experienced some sort of trauma in their lives—they were abused, their mothers died, they came down with tuberculosis. So, suddenly, only about twenty of our students were able to pass that exam. These are environmental circumstances that we deal with daily, things that we can't control or anticipate. If you are working with someone who has inflexible parameters for defining success, you're in jeopardy of losing vital grant funding. Donors need to be partners, and it goes both ways. We tell them exactly what's happening with our programs—what's working, what's not—and in turn we expect that they'll understand that you can't raise a child in a twelve-month grant cycle. If you find donors who believe in the long-term goal, and you as an organization are willing to trust your donors, to be honest with them, and to engage with them about what happened and what the next steps are, a situation such as the one we faced doesn't have to be an insurmountable setback.

First, we had those twenty students who passed an important exam. Then, because we are committed to the community and invested in it, we could put resources toward working with those families that were homeless so they could regain their footing and the students could think about the exam next year. For the children going through other types of trauma, we had staff who were able to work closely with them, to support them however they needed, to make sure they got the necessary medical help, and to give them food or clothing or whatever they needed to stay afloat.

This situation demonstrates perfectly, too, why the development world's obsession with overhead, and what constitutes overhead, strikes me as absurd. Dan Palotta, the activist and AIDS Ride founder, articulated the attitude perfectly in his TED talk "The Way We Think about Charity Is Dead Wrong."

> *So in the for-profit sector, the more value you produce, the more money you can make. But we don't like nonprofits to use money to incentivize people to produce more in social service. We have a visceral reaction to the idea that anyone would make very much money helping other people. Interesting that we don't have a visceral reaction to the notion that people would make a lot of money not helping other people. You know, you want to make fifty million dollars selling violent video games to kids, go for it. We'll put you on the cover of Wired magazine. But you want to make half a million dollars trying to cure kids of malaria, and you're considered a parasite yourself.*

We need good human beings to interact with our kids. What is a staff person's salary if not a program cost? Everything Ubuntu does is about one person sitting with a child to tutor her, someone else sitting with that child to counsel her, another person sitting with the child to go over medical issues—it's all about human interaction.

So, yes, our programs are expensive—an average of $5,000 per year to put a child on a pathway out of poverty. To many people who were raised on the idea that only a dollar a day will save a child's life, that sounds excessive. But the money is out there. Billions of dollars are being invested in Africa each year, and it's no secret that the results are not amazing. With all this aid money, why aren't more leaders being produced, why aren't more kids in these impoverished areas getting into top universities? Maybe it's because we're giving them a cup of soup, a windup computer, and a shipping container for a school.

~~~~~~~

In 2002, I became friends with a teacher at Frederick Douglass Academy II in Harlem whose name was Latasha Greer. We came up with the idea of creating a cultural exchange program in which we would take eight seventh-graders from Harlem, eight from Port Elizabeth, and three teachers from each school and create a shared curriculum drawing parallels between the antiapartheid movement in South America and the civil rights movement in the United States. We got $50,000 from the office of New York Congressman Charles Rangel to fund the program. We called it the Young Ambassadors Program.

Nearly all of the students who'd been in Gcobani's poetry club, including Lwando, transitioned to the Young Ambassadors Program after demonstrating their seriousness of purpose with community service work and speeches on social activism. Gcobani and Jana ran the program for us, while Latasha ran it on the Harlem side. Jana spent hours preparing the students for their trip to New York—having them practice their speeches, talking about the cultural differences to expect and how to react to them. Gcobani guided them through the curriculum: The students were reading speeches given by Mahatma Gandhi, Martin Luther King Jr., and Nelson Mandela, looking at the influence of one on another. The New York and South African students would exchange letters, trading thoughts on the reading and experiences in their own lives; I often carried the students' letters with me as I traveled back and forth, because the mail was slow and sometimes unreliable.

The Harlem students traveled to Port Elizabeth in 2003. They all came from tough neighborhoods in New York, and many of them had never been outside of the United States before. They stayed in their pen pals' homes in the townships, and I think they were overwhelmed by seeing the way so many people live here. No running water, no electricity, in tiny houses crowded with eight or nine people each night. On the first day we were all together, the American students were on one side of the room, the Ubuntu students on the other—pretty typical middle school cliquishness. I'd anticipated as much, so the next day we went out to the Baviaanskloof nature reserve for a five-day camping trip. Everyone had to work together, fording rivers and passing the bags across, setting up our campsite each night. Very quickly, all boundaries broke down.

At the end of the first day, we camped on the sandy shore of a river. Latasha and I were sitting up on the bank, watching her students and ours play in the water, sixteen thirteen-year-olds splashing each other, laughing, acting silly. For the first time, I saw all the similarities between these children, not their differences. Latasha said quietly, "Jake, I've never seen our kids just be children before."

~~~~~~~

The process of getting our students ready to visit New York was arduous, and Jana and Gcobani worked ceaselessly to get everything done. Many of the students didn't have any official paperwork, many didn't have parents, and Ubuntu had to take over the process of registering them with the government. One student, Sipho, had been abandoned by his mother and beaten so badly by his stepfather that he was nearly blind in one eye. Soon after he started attending the poetry club, we discovered that he had enormous welts across his back; his stepfather had wanted him to go play sports instead of staying in to read. Many of the kids we work with can be manipulative in a certain way—when it's a matter of survival, you learn how to be a salesman. But Sipho was always sincere, always quiet, always sweet and serious.

Sipho didn't have a birth certificate, and, without his mother, we had little chance of getting one. Sipho was convinced that there was no way he would get a passport in time for the trip. But Gcobani told him, despite having no real plan, "Don't worry, we're going to make it happen." He spent days persuading Sipho's stepfather to help him, and discovered an aunt living not far away who could vouch for his birthplace. Gcobani drove them to the ministry to provide verification, and in a matter of days, Sipho had a passport in his hands: his first official government document.

At last, all eight of the Young Ambassadors were on the plane to New York that May. We had an incredible three weeks in the city, and in some ways it was overwhelming for the students. Vincent and Anne Mai, longtime supporters of Ubuntu, arranged a private tour of the American Museum of Natural History and then took everyone out to dinner. Vincent asked me, "What do they like to eat?" I told him, "Our kids love meat." So we went to a New York steakhouse, one of those places that charges $40 a steak. These students were used to having a tiny piece of goat, when they had meat at all, and here each one of them had a steak the size of their head in front of them, a huge platter of roasted potatoes to share, all the bread they could eat. By the time we were done, every thirteen-year-old was terribly sick.

Along with the Harlem students, we also met with several of our board members and donors in their offices, where they talked to the students about their experiences in the professional world. We wanted them to be exposed to successful men and women who had something in common with their background, so they could see what kind of achievement was possible for them. Everywhere we went, Lwando would break out his impeccable Mandela impersonation.

A few days after our steak dinner, Vincent invited us up to his office on the fiftieth floor of a building in Midtown, where he told them about growing up on a farm in the Eastern Cape, not far from Port Elizabeth, and then coming to work in New York's financial industry. Sipho listened carefully to Vincent, looked around the large, comfortable corporate office, the nice furniture, Vincent's big desk, and said thoughtfully, "You know what I want to be when I grow up? A chartered accountant."

The head of Motown Records, who described his rise from a life of poverty in Brooklyn to the executive office, also hosted us. He warned them about fantasizing about easy wealth, describing the way that a million-dollar record deal gets whittled down by the fees of lawyers, agents, all the people who support a musician in business. He wasn't discouraging—he emphasized needing, in any industry, to slow down, find mentors who can help you, make sure you have all the information you need to make decisions. He dazzled all the students with everything from his life story to his office lined with gold records.

Our final event was a benefit breakfast at the Penn Club of New York, the first time we'd had the opportunity to bring students we were working with to the people who gave us money. We wanted to thank our supporters, and to give them a chance to get to know the children whose lives they were affecting. Every student and every teacher made a speech. Looking back, maybe it was a bit much, but it did bring our programs to life for the people who had believed in us all these years.

〜〜〜〜〜

We ran the Young Ambassadors Program for only one year. It was an intensive program that cost a lot in money, time, and resources, and Ubuntu simply couldn't afford it at that time. We were still finding our feet as an organization, and I could see that the time we were spending on these eight students was detracting from some of our other efforts. Jana and Gcobani, in particular, had devoted themselves to these students and ground themselves down in order to give them individualized attention while managing other projects as well. Yet the program was a remarkable success: Out of sixteen high-risk children, thirteen went on to university.

You sometimes hear people in business say that simple is good. I think that's what happened here. Yes, there was a lot of programming involved in Young Ambassadors, and clearly the overseas trip required massive logistical work. But fundamentally, Young Ambassadors was about showing love and attention to a small group of kids in an intense environment. They had three teachers for eight kids, every day of the trip. None of these students had received such dedicated care and nurturing before.

Most of the South African students stayed with us through high school and into university. Sipho was accepted to one of the best schools in South Africa, the University of Cape Town, but he chose to go to school in Port Elizabeth so he could stay close to Ubuntu, and interned with us each afternoon after school. Now he's pursuing a master's in sociology while undertaking an internship in human relations. Lwando graduated from the University of Cape Town and joined the communications and marketing department of that university. Nozibele, one of several siblings being raised by a single mother, was one of our first students to graduate from university. She was immediately hired for a marketing job at Continental Tire, and then traveled to Germany for a training program in management; in all, she spent a year abroad. When she came back, she rejoined Ubuntu as an external relations manager, eager to make her own impact on the community.

What's most difficult is seeing the ones who don't make it. Fufu was a young girl who, despite her sunny smile and cheerful demeanor, harbored a lot of sadness. Her mom had died, and she lived with an aunt in the township. Of all the kids in the Young Ambassadors, she was the most obviously vulnerable and innocent. When we came back from New York, we dropped each child off at his or her home. When we got to Fufu's home, her aunt was no longer there. No one could tell us where she was, or if she was coming back.

Gcobani took Fufu to his home, where she stayed for several weeks until one day her aunt reappeared. She moved back in with the aunt, but the situation was unstable. Fufu started to miss her after-school programming, stopped showing up at school, began avoiding us. Then, over Christmas in 2006, she disappeared. We tried to find her, but she wanted to be lost. We'd hear about her from time to time, that she'd begun working on the streets, but we weren't able to bring her back to Ubuntu.

〜〜〜〜〜

"Jake, you've got to meet this amazing family," Jordan told me over the phone one day in 2006. I was back in New York for a few weeks, and between Jordan and Jana, I'd heard constantly about this incredible girl named Zethu who was taking care of her younger siblings, Star and Lungi.

"Okay, I'll go visit them, I promise," I told him.

I flew into Port Elizabeth the next week. Fezeka, Zethu's case manager, met me at the office and we made our way to the Kwandokwenza Hostel, one of the brick complexes that had been built during apartheid to house migrant workers. Now families lived there, crowded together into small rooms with communal kitchens, living rooms, and bathrooms. The doors had no locks, and no security measures were in place. Rape and child abuse were endemic.

The first thing I saw was a young, petite girl standing under a single lightbulb, industriously sawing at a giant cabbage with a knife that was clearly too dull for the job. She was still in her school uniform. Her younger brother, Star, was standing next to her, watching her work.

"This is Zethu," Fezeka said.

Zethu turned to me with a quick smile, and I saw immediately what had drawn so many people in. Despite the circumstances, she illuminated the room with her confident charisma and evident strength.

Fezeka had told me the story of Zethu's family on our way there. Her father had died of an HIV-related illness in 2004. The family wore their mourning clothes, as tradition dictated, for a year. Two months later, her mother died, also of an illness related to HIV. Zethu was fourteen. She had two younger siblings: her brother, Star, who was eleven, and her sister, Lungi, who was nine. They moved in with their aunt and cousins in a shack in New Brighton for a time. A few months later, their aunt accepted a job in Johannesburg and couldn't take them with them. Soon Zethu and her siblings moved into a room at the hostel, on their own.

Zethu had been involved with Ubuntu since she was eleven; she'd attended computer class at her school, B. J. Mnyanda, and attended other workshops and camps through middle school. After three months of struggling with her parents' deaths, Zethu drew one of the Ubuntu counselors aside and told her that she and her siblings were orphaned and needed help. Within days, all three children were enrolled as Ubuntu clients, taken to see a doctor, and given food packets. We also installed locks on their door.

Until HIV/AIDS swept South Africa, the concept of being orphaned was almost unknown. Extended families ensured that, even if something happened to a child's parents, that child would be taken care of by a grandmother, an aunt, a cousin. But, suddenly, this awful virus caused families to splinter. When I'd walk around the township, I'd suddenly realize that my generation had been decimated. The men and women who came of age after 1994—most of them had died, and they'd left behind young families. You began to see a ten- or twelve-year-old suddenly become head of a household, not only fending for herself, but also caring for her siblings. In part, it was a fear of infection or of stigma that made their relatives reluctant to take them in, but, more pressingly, many relatives simply didn't have the resources to take care of them. We'd often see a situation where one woman would have her own children and one or more siblings' children: eleven people or more in one small house, with no income. Township cemeteries, acres and acres of land, were being filled beyond capacity. In the flimsy shacks that surrounded them, the children left behind struggled to keep themselves alive.

CHANGING THE CONVERSATION: SETTING A PRICE TAG ON A CHILD

THE SCENARIO: I'M meeting an executive in his Park Avenue penthouse office. He leans over his polished desk and asks me earnestly, "How many kids can I get for $10,000?" It's an all-too-common conversation when fund-raising for an organization that works in Africa.

But think, for a moment, about everything it took to get you where you are today. Think about all the textbooks, classes, tutors, soccer games, music lessons, and doctors' visits. Think about all the love and support you received from your family, friends, and teachers. Now think about how your experience was unique and inherently different from that of a friend or sibling. Parenting is individualized and responsive—what works for you might not work for someone else.

The challenges that people living in abject poverty face are equally unique and arguably more complicated than our own. Some parents must choose between buying their children's textbooks and feeding their families, while others may have children who are too sick to focus on their studies. Some students struggle with reading, while their peers who can easily memorize vocabulary experience recurring psychological abuse at home. There is no single proven remedy that can be replicated across all contexts. Instead, there is only an understanding that all children have different, equally important needs.

Given all these challenges, we've determined that it takes an average of $5,000 per year to set a child on a pathway out of poverty, and in early childhood it can be upward of $11,000. It's not actually that much, when you compare it to the average cost to raise a child in the United States, or even elsewhere in South Africa. But I still hear it all the time: "We like what you're doing, but how do you reach more children for less money?" Every time, I tell them they should rethink the question. It shouldn't be how you do more with less, but how much it costs to change a child's life.

—

Jacob Harold is the president and CEO of GuideStar, which has gathered 2.5 billion pieces of data about nonprofits that are used by seven million people each year. Before joining GuideStar, Harold oversaw the Philanthropy Program of the William and Flora Hewlett Foundation; earlier in his career, he

(continued)

also worked for the Rainforest Action Network, Greenpeace USA, and the David and Lucile Packard Foundation. He frequently writes on philanthropic strategy and climate change.

When deciding on what nonprofit to donate to, what factors do most people consider? What matters to them? What matters to you, personally?

HAROLD: Well, we need to start with the issue: What is the social or environmental issue that you care about? And then, I think we should have one goal: Maximize the potential good per dollar without being a jerk. Let me explain. All good work rests on an ethical foundation and so that rules out being a jerk. And I say "potential" because we must recognize that social change is hard and there are no guarantees—and it must be okay for nonprofits to take risks. "Per dollar" is important because a donor or an organization with more money simply has a greater responsibility. The hard concept, then, is "maximizing good"—there is simply no simple, easy way to measure social good. But that doesn't mean we shouldn't try.

What factors should donors consider when thinking about the money they are investing? How can we redirect that conversation?

HAROLD: Well, to start out, it's good that you said "factors" plural—because there are many. But if I had to pick a first one to consider, it would be this: clarity. How clear is a nonprofit about its goals and strategies? Clarity goes a long way toward ensuring the smart and effective use of limited resources. Next is feedback: Does the nonprofit have a way to learn if it's on the right track and to make midcourse corrections? A few basic measurement tools and regular conversations with stakeholders go a long way toward helping an organization learn from and react to a constantly changing world.

And, indeed, the opinions of stakeholders can be a great proxy for performance. If the homeless people at a homeless shelter all rave about the management of the shelter, that's a very good sign. And if journalists that cover Congress all think a nonprofit is influential, it probably is.

Do you feel that people still subscribe to the notion that you can "save a child for a dollar per day"?

HAROLD: Well, there certainly are some donors who do; otherwise, it wouldn't continue as a fund-raising strategy. But if you ask anyone who has done serious work to address poverty, they'll say it's a dangerous oversimplification of how change actually happens in the world.

Why do you think that people have, however abstractly or loosely, an idea about how much it takes to "save" or "transform" the life of a child in, say, Africa? Where do you think that number comes from?

HAROLD: Well, the thing about oversimplifications is that they tend to be easy to remember. And being easy to remember is one of the essential characteristics of a good marketing strategy. The dollar-a-day approach is not a social change strategy; it's a marketing strategy. There are good organizations that have used that frame to raise money. And I get that, it's hard to raise money. But that doesn't change the fact that it has sowed confusion among donors.

The number people find reasonable to spend on a child elsewhere is often much lower than what an American family spends to raise a child. Where do you think this disparity comes from? Why do you think that this disconnect exists? Why would it be so much "cheaper" to raise a child in Africa?

HAROLD: Our common humanity has been filtered through many different histories. That may seem obvious, but we too often forget that those histories have consequences. Africa is still dealing with the legacy of colonialism; indeed, we are all still dealing with the legacy of colonialism. And our challenge is to never forget that amidst all this complexity, all human lives are equally valuable.

That's the moral or historical answer. But there's also an arithmetic answer. People don't always do the math. They know that some things are cheaper in Africa, and so the idea of a dollar a day is somehow believable. But as anyone who has built the budget of an organization addressing poverty in Africa knows, those numbers simply don't add up. When we take seriously that all human lives are equally valuable, it's easy to see that real change costs more than pocket change.

Do you think this mentality is problematic? How can we change it?

HAROLD: It's definitely problematic. But it's also understandable. Not everyone gets to visit Africa or study economics or is exposed to the richness of our crazy world. We have to deal with oversimplifications, but "dealing" doesn't just mean we sit back and relax. We need an intentional effort to offer alternatives to donors.

(continued)

How has the philanthropic environment changed over the past ten or twenty years? What questions do you hear now that are new? What do you think accounts for these changes, if any?

HAROLD: I'm glad to say there have been some very promising changes over the last couple of decades. There's so much more data available now about nonprofits, about poverty, about what works. As people—donors, nonprofit executives, beneficiaries, journalists—get used to having access to that data, they're asking much better questions about effectiveness, about learning, about feedback. We have a lot of work ahead of us, but I'm optimistic the conversation is going to get a lot smarter. And that's just what we need to get real results.

CHAPTER SEVEN

Our Mission Is the Same, Now Let's Change Everything Else

Early each morning, Zethu would wake up and start preparing for the day. She'd go get a pot of water and warm it, so that she and her siblings could take turns washing up. They didn't have a bathroom, so they'd use a corner of their shared room to bathe. Once Zethu finished her bath, she'd start ironing each of their uniforms, making sure that they were in good condition for school. Then they walked to school together.

When she returned home, Zethu would give her brother and sister some steam bread—a little like a dumpling—to tide them over until dinner, and then start preparing whatever they had for an evening meal. Often, she'd have a whole cabbage to stretch out over four days. Then they would lie down in the same room where they washed, ironed, ate, and studied, and go to sleep for the night.

During holidays, the children would also attend camps, where they'd participate in drama, write poetry, learn about health, or take computer courses. It was a way for the children to escape from their day-to-day reality, to simply be kids. "I remember the first camp," Lungi, Zethu's sister, told me. "I've never been in such an amazing environment, with people you love and people who love you back. You can forget what's troubling you outside, you forget about the bad things and have fun and learn and learn. I think we were given a chance to find ourselves there."

Zethu took her role as the head of the household seriously. Early on, she showed Fezeka the paperwork her mother had left documenting her application for a house built under the Reconstruction and Development Programm; these low-cost homes were gradually replacing shacks in the townships, offering still small and basic but sturdier accommodation. Fezeka and Gcobani took Zethu, along with all the paperwork, to the ward counselor to make sure that the Ngceza children got the home that their mother had wanted to provide for them.

Sometimes, of course, Star and Lungi chafed at Zethu's mothering. Lungi, smart, spirited, and independent, often tested her limits. Each December, the siblings would go to the Transkei, the rural homeland where some of their extended family still lived, during the school break. One year, Zethu told Lungi to start to get ready to make the trip, and Lungi responded, "No, I want to spend time with my friends in Port Elizabeth."

Zethu looked at her as sternly as she could manage and said, "No, I'm telling you."

Lungi shot back, "No, I'm telling *you*, I'm not going there." As Zethu recalls ruefully, "Sometimes I'd win, sometimes I'd lose."

Many times, Zethu recalled, when Lungi or Star became upset by Zethu's instructions, they'd tell her, "No, ma'am, you are not my mother, you are my sister." It cut Zethu to the quick, because she was trying so hard to be their mother. "I would get angry at them saying that, as if it was an insult," she remembers. "But it was the truth."

As our goals as an organization started to solidify around the idea of serving the whole child, not isolated needs, our senior leadership began to take shape as well. Jordan and Jana had continued to be instrumental in the evolution of Ubuntu, and their roles quickly grew to reflect their energy and passion. Jordan took over the role of chief operating officer and ran much of the day-to-day work in South Africa, while Jana worked on our programming and scholarship efforts, and on refining our monitoring and evaluation system. She spent hours with administrators, counselors, and students, figuring out what worked, what we needed to do better, where our energy made the most difference.

One thing Jordan did was force me to look at our organization very realistically and very honestly in a way I'd never done before. I tend to set a goal and charge forward without thinking about whether the people I'm taking with me want to or need to work at breakneck speed fifteen hours a day. We were growing, from a dozen employees to nearly fifty, and he helped me see that not everyone was in it for the same reasons I was, and that that was okay. I had to be aware of my role as the founder of the organization, that whatever I said or how I acted with one employee would set a precedent. And as we grew, I couldn't keep trying to have my finger on every decision, every piece of paper that came through the office, and every person we hired and trained.

His role, like those of so many others at the time, encompassed much more than his title suggested. He spent a lot of time with our financial team, with our external relations efforts, and with HR. One year, he sat in on every performance evaluation in the entire organization in South Africa—at the time, about three dozen individuals. It took an enormous amount of time and energy, but he came out of it with a personal understanding of and connection with every single person who worked for us in Port Elizabeth. Today, we're big enough of an organization that a task like this would be impossible, but then it offered a vital snapshot of Ubuntu.

Jana's path was more circuitous, and more difficult. She worked extremely hard every day, but people looked at her and saw her as a white American woman and Jordan's girlfriend. Her ideas for change were often seen as disrespectful, or personally hurtful. While Jordan quickly took on an official, visible role in the senior leadership, Jana's role was more nebulous, and she often became frustrated at what seemed to her to be a boy's club—Jordan, Banks, Gcobani, Qondakele, and me—making the final decisions.* I compounded her frustration by seeming to ignore or discount the real tension that had grown in the office, and our relationship frayed.

Another strong woman, Tarryn Mthimkhulu, soon joined Ubuntu, though her shyness initially disguised her tenacity and dedication. Tarryn arrived for her interview for a bookkeeping position just off a seventeen-hour bus ride from Johannesburg. Jordan picked her up. When she got into his car, she immediately made a phone call and spent the trip to the office on her cell, which irritated Jordan. Later, he realized that she was so painfully shy that she couldn't bear the idea of trying to make conversation. Tarryn spent a couple of hours in the office and gave an impressive interview, and then got right back on the bus to Johannesburg. When she was hired, she had nowhere to live in Port Elizabeth, so Gcobani said, "Oh, you can stay with my aunt." It was the kind of gesture that characterized Ubuntu: If someone needed a home, you offered her one.

At first, Tarryn was unsure what exactly she had taken on. "I had my doubts that I made the right choice in coming here, because you guys just stuck me in the corner with a box of papers," she remembered. "It was noisy, I wasn't used to working in an open space, and everyone shouted across the room at each other. I just worked quietly in my corner." But as she settled in and saw the challenge and the opportunity

---

* It should be said: Four amazing women each spent years on the leadership committee at various times before moving on to other organizations. These women—Lungi Fatwela, Annika Millhouse, Ann Magege, and Phumla Mnyanda—made a profound impact on Ubuntu.

ahead of her, she realized that she could make a difference in the organization, and that excited her. The accepting atmosphere also made her happy. "Ubuntu allows me to be me," she told me. "I don't have to conform to a certain conception of how you have to be if you are an accountant."

Jordan, as her supervisor, noticed Tarryn's immediate impact on the way Ubuntu's finances were kept. Tarryn approached her work with deadly honesty and total transparency. She not only made sure we reported our expenses thoroughly and accurately but also fiercely protected our resources. In many ways, Tarryn is the best and the brightest of South Africa. Perhaps more than anyone else on my leadership team, she could have gone to a corporate job and excelled, both professionally and monetarily. But she turned down all offers in order to stay with us, because she believed so strongly in what we were doing, and in her place in that work. "To this day, it's not about money," Tarryn told me recently. "It's that I'm happy every day coming to work."

As Tarryn grew comfortable in her financial role, she also found ways to be a leader in HR and other policy areas. At the time, it was both a strength and a weakness of our leadership team that there was so much ambiguity about our roles. For Jana and Tarryn, it meant that they could take over large areas of leadership, because they had the passion and the energy and the ability, and there were no lines drawn saying that they couldn't. But it also meant that it was a struggle for them to get recognized for the work they were doing—and often, even to do the work that they saw needed to get done.

Qondakele, meanwhile, continued to develop within the organization. He was a key member of our leadership team, and his charisma and charm made him a vital part of our community outreach. If a community member or a donor had an issue with us, we knew to send Qondakele. He soon moved from project manager to director of initiatives, and then, as our first group of students started to consider university, he began to develop our higher education program, including establishing scholarships and support beyond the townships.

My role was to keep all these strong personalities and passionate workers moving in the same direction. I had to make sure that Ubuntu continued to have a clear mission, and that meant managing everyone else's anxieties and frustrations. Every conflict and difficulty among the senior leadership came to me; every question and fear that anyone had—about their own career, about our programs, about the future of the organization—all these were directed at me. My vision of our work had to keep us moving steadily forward, and I worked hard to balance all the personalities, to provide reassurance, and to motivate each person toward the goal. It was a huge amount of pressure on me, and it was a very real problem: I knew that if I wasn't there, Ubuntu wouldn't exist. I considered the fact that the organization was so Jake-centric one of my greatest failures.

But one of my great accomplishments was to surround myself with brilliant people and let them do the work they did best. Banks, Gcobani, Jordan, Jana, Qondakele, and Tarryn all had skills I lacked, and I had to let go of parts of Ubuntu and let them do the things I couldn't. We all knew that every decision, every argument over the direction we were taking or a program we wanted to implement, happened because we all cared deeply about what we were doing. No one had a personal agenda that was influencing his or her decisions, and that made an enormous difference in our leadership team. And what drew us and everyone else together was the intensity of the work we were doing. Every day, we dealt with death, with rape, with abuse, with illness and malnutrition, and it wore on us. You can't endure that with someone and not develop a deep respect and love for the other person.

And over time, it became abundantly clear that we all had our roles, and that Ubuntu would not succeed without each one of us. I had a strategic vision, and the energy and the drive to demand that we keep growing and improving. Banks had amazing relationships within the community that kept us connected to the people we were serving.

Gcobani, in every action and word, embodied the spirit of *ubuntu*, the total recognition of others' humanity. Jordan created order out of chaos, and provided management to execute the vision of the organization. Qondakele cared deeply about our mission, and his personal conviction was contagious to the community and to donors. Jana had absolute passion for the on-the-ground programs, rigorously making sure that what we did was effective for the children we worked with. And Tarryn gave Ubuntu financial solidity, ensured the long-term viability of our programs, and acted as a calm counterbalance to us all.

~~~~~~

A few external factors created changes in our organization, as well. In 2002, I'd met a South African doctor named Frank Lipman, who practices integrative medicine at his Eleven Eleven Wellness Center in Manhattan. He'd founded a group called Nomadocs, comprised of doctors and healers who traveled to different areas of the world to provide free health care. He asked to come down with his group to see if we could collaborate on a program of urban organic gardens. By the end of the visit, Frank had decided to liquidate his group and donate all their money to us to run our own gardening and wellness initiative, and he became one of our board members.

We hired Mava Dlepu, who had worked in South Africa's Department of Agriculture, Forestry, and Fisheries helping small farmers compete commercially, to develop a food security program. Around this time, my brother, Matthew, moved down to Port Elizabeth as well, and became involved in the gardening program; he had a degree in agriculture and had recently spent time in Havana, which has an extensive network of community gardens. It was supposed to be a six-month volunteer position; he ended up staying for five years.

Matt has always been a character. Jordan remembers Matt sitting on my parents' front porch at four years old, holding a sign that read, "CONVERSATIONS ABOUT GOD: 50 CENTS." (He'd been inspired by his favorite *Peanuts* cartoon.) At Ubuntu, he'd work hard, but more often than not he'd disappear without warning and reappear hours later with a whole goat over his shoulder. He'd studied to be a chef in Paris, and he'd pull together herbs and spices and cook up the goat for the whole office to share. Suddenly, we were having a gourmet meal in the middle of the townships.

The community garden initiative became an important component of our programs. Over time, we established gardens at clinics, at primary schools, in individuals' backyards, and at Ubuntu itself.

Around this time we also moved again, to a former doctor's office at 5 Qeqe Street, in the heart of Zwide township. The office was a big cement and brick building set back from a large empty lot. When we bought it, a man lived in the empty lot in a repurposed container; I was told that he came with the property. He lived there for more than three years before we eventually negotiated to move the container for him, at no small cost to us. Students painted a vivid mural on one side of our brick building and we planted gardens in the lot; goats would often wander in and eat our plants, so we took turns on goat duty to chase them away. Jordan and Banks had painted the inside of the office a bright lime green, hoping it would be cheerful, but it turned out to be putrid, and there were no windows, no fans, and only one bathroom for nearly sixty employees. We had no conference room, so meetings were held outside in a gazebo in the empty lot. But despite its problems, the space felt huge to us, and we never thought we'd outgrow it.

Most significantly, the United States President's Emergency Plan for AIDS Relief (PEPFAR), which launched in 2003, allowed Ubuntu to access millions of dollars for our health education and outreach programs. We were amazed at the extent of the program. In 2006, we received a grant for $4.5 million over five years; suddenly, our budget grew by nearly 20 percent. Along with that came much more stringent and structured reporting requirements, because the money was allocated for specific programs that had to meet certain standards and achieve certain goals. It forced us to adapt in significant ways from our familial beginnings. Five years later, we decided to turn down the PEPFAR funding, as it no longer made sense in the context of our programs. We'd developed programs to satisfy PEPFAR requirements that were worthy endeavors but, ultimately, weren't serving our core mission. By the end, we'd started to call it drug money: It was exciting and sexy, but it would eventually kill us.

However, the money from PEPFAR forced us into a structure of reporting and accountability that, while feeling at times uncomfortably corporate for a grassroots organization, also pressed us into setting and attaining high professional standards for ourselves. Just because we weren't making a profit didn't mean we couldn't strive for quality and excellence. We shy away from the word "charity" for that reason. "Charity" implies a certain degradation of standards; often, the person giving becomes more important than the person receiving. We talk about what we do as "development": We are working to help build a community, and ultimately to help build a new nation, to fill the needs of the people who live here, and to foster skills and jobs to create long-term stability. It's all part of the goal Banks and I set out with: to empower young people with the skills to succeed economically and within the social structure so that they can provide their own families with successful futures.

Part of this philosophy, too, comes through in our relationships with our donors. We don't see this as an adversarial relationship, one in which we want something from them, and they want something from us, and we're both trying to give as little as possible. We see our donors as partners. We want them to feel like they are a part of Ubuntu, and we want them to fully understand what we do. When I meet a potential donor, I'm not in a rush to get their money. I want to talk to them, make sure that they buy in to our long-term vision. Donors truly become friends, and these relationships last for years.

～～～～～

One very difficult decision we wrestled with during this time was whether or not to stay in the schools. We all had seen, over the six years we'd been working inside the schools, that incompetence, poor training, bureaucracy, and a lack of incentive to change impeded our progress with the children we were trying to reach. We were spending an inordinate amount of time negotiating with principals and teachers, trying to urge them toward getting more training, working to secure their buy-in on our programs and our ideas. And too often it didn't get us anywhere. The resources we were pouring in—the computer centers and libraries and the expertise to run them—couldn't have the impact we wanted in the highly dysfunctional institutions that hosted them. Unions had the power to cripple the whole province overnight, and they inhibited any kind of change. Fundamentally, we had no way to hold teachers accountable. They were government employees, not ours, and we didn't have any real carrots or sticks with which to motivate them. And if you don't have any accountability, you can't make any progress.

Jana started to push us toward leaving the schools and toward a model of working directly with children and their families. It didn't take long for her to convince Jordan, and the two of them began working on me. From the very beginning, the inefficiency of working in the schools had been apparent to me. But our founding vision to help get township children to stable health, a stable home, and, eventually, a stable income had always relied on a strategy of working within the school structure and reforming education in the township from the inside out. Would we be compromising our integrity as an organization, or completely altering our mission, if we left the schools? Or would we be accelerating our ability to achieve our mission?

It seemed apparent that we would be more effective if we integrated the education piece of our work with our health, nutrition, and household stability programs. I knew, intellectually, that this was a step we needed to take; emotionally, I wrestled with it. But as the senior leadership looked at example after example of the schools' hindering our work—computer labs being underutilized, hours of staff time devoted to training that teachers never put into practice—I realized there was no way that our organization could seriously change these institutions. The dysfunction and lack of accountability are so deep-rooted that there's no way to solve it from the bottom up. And I became convinced that this was a necessary evolution of our mission, not a break from it.

But Banks and Gcobani were teachers who were entrenched in the very school system that we were now convinced was completely nonfunctional. Our indictment of the schools could be felt as an indictment of their work. They'd both grown up in the townships, where schools, one of the few social services provided, were seen as sacrosanct. And both Gcobani and Banks had long, deeply rooted relationships in the community, and much of the buy-in Ubuntu had received over the years was the direct result of their promises to the community. They never made an explicit pledge to work in the schools, but there was certainly an implicit understanding that we would.

The process took a long time, as we spent hours as a senior leadership group discussing this change, what it would mean for Ubuntu, how we would continue to reach these children, and what our programs would look like on the other side. More than a year went by as we pushed and pulled and debated each point; we never really argued, but there was tension in the room. Gcobani became convinced that this was the right direction to take.

Banks, though, had a harder time believing that we would be able to stay true to our original mission if we weren't in the schools. He pointed out that regardless of whether the computer centers and libraries were as effective as we wanted them to be, they represented something larger: It was the first time anyone had put computers, or an organized library, into township schools. We had been pioneers, and we'd seen the difference it made for the children to have high-quality resources in their own schools. It provided a spark to their imagination: What else was out there for them?

Banks also had a bigger personal stake as well. He was the face of Ubuntu to much of the community; if people resented our pulling out of the schools, he would be the focus of their displeasure. There was a long period of time when I thought Banks might leave Ubuntu over this.

Eventually, he realized that we couldn't keep going the way we were. We'd gone over every aspect of this transition a dozen times, and he was 99 percent convinced, but there was still a small part of him holding back. One day, I took him aside and promised him that this would work, and that this would be the best way to keep our integrity and serve our mission. He looked almost relieved. "You can't give people things and then hold their hands until the end," he told me. "And it looked like we were going to hold hands to the end."

Of course, we didn't abruptly pull out one day; it took another two years of meetings, during which we assured the community that we would still provide services for the children. Many of the teachers were angry, and it wasn't an entirely smooth process. But the children we worked with largely transferred into our client-directed services without a hiccup.

This was the start of what we now call our pathway. It is a way to ensure that each child we work with, and their family, is enrolled in an individualized, comprehensive array of services to help them reach adulthood and a career: nutritional support, health services, tutoring, summer camps, and counseling and support groups. Difficult as it was, breaking with the schools was a major turning point for Ubuntu, one that let us become what we needed to be.

CHANGING THE CONVERSATION: INVESTING IN "OVERHEAD"

THE INDUSTRY OVERHEAD standard in nonprofits is less than 20 percent. How do we do it? Most of the time, organizations rely on a mixture of three strategies: a) understaffing, using outdated technology, and declining to make the long-term investments in infrastructure that would ultimately strengthen the organization; b) reallocating staff salaries, technological costs, and spending on financial oversight to disguise the true costs of overhead; or c) using the marketing strategy of promising that 100 percent of a donor's dollars go to programs, because the board will cover overhead costs. Once an organization has undermined itself and underreported its actual costs, it uses the lower number to prove its effectiveness to new donors. This strategy leads donors to expect that organizations can always manage with less. It's a vicious cycle, and it's unnecessary.

There are two sides of the overhead conversation. On the one hand, people ask me all the time why we spend so much on staff salaries. I tell them, "Ask me instead how much impact we are having." Without excellent staff our counselors, our household stability specialists, our tutors, our early-childhood educators, our pharmacist, our financial team, our gardener—what does Ubuntu have? Our staff *is* our programming, and we need to pay them a competitive salary with strong benefits and proper training.

Overhead allows us to innovate—to invest in the infrastructure of our organization so that we can continue to grow. With starved systems, those nonprofits trying to squeak by on less than 20 percent would be unable to take advantage of a growth in fund-raising.

And that's the second major strain of criticism we see concerning overhead. I've sat down with donors and had them question why we'd spent over $900,000 on fund-raising. What they didn't ask was "How much did you produce with that money?" We have a consistently high return on our fund-raising costs, typically returning anywhere from one to six dollars for every dollar we spend. In the for-profit world, that would make us a big success. But in the nonprofit world, judgment is predicated on the absolute value of what is spent, rather than on what that money generates.

Dan Pallotta, in his 2013 TED talk, addresses this discrepancy perfectly:

(continued)

So we've all been taught that charities should spend as little as possible on overhead things like fund-raising under the theory that, well, the less money you spend on fund-raising, the more money there is available for the cause. Well, that's true if it's a depressing world in which this pie cannot be made any bigger. But if it's a logical world in which investment in fundraising actually raises more funds and makes the pie bigger, then we have it precisely backwards, and we should be investing more money, not less, in fund-raising, because fund-raising is the one thing that has the potential to multiply the amount of money available for the cause that we care about so deeply.

It's a common question: "You spend an average of $5,000 a child. But could you do it for $4,000?" Why aren't they saying to us, "What if you spent $10,000?" Imagine the impact if we could spend twice as much. Or, maybe it *wouldn't* double. But shouldn't the possibility be part of the conversation? What if we spent more—would we have that much greater of an impact? Could we raise that kind of money? These are valuable questions, but the vast majority of people focus only on doing it cheaper.

When you look at the for-profit sector, it's clear why this is such a strange demand. Much of what in nonprofits is defined as overhead is defined as research and development in for-profits. These costs are the engine that keeps a company running, innovating, staying relevant. If Apple got audited the way Ubuntu does and overhead was defined for them in the same way it is for us, you'd see an enormous percentage of their money going to overhead.

We must choose to shift these donor expectations; we must decide for ourselves to invest in overhead and be brave enough to refuse funding that undermines our ability to innovate. Because who else will? Nonprofits have to be bolder. We have to start thinking about our relationship with supporters as more than a one-sided pitch for funding. With years of experience working to reduce poverty, we must educate donors. We have a responsibility to shift their mentalities, to share the lessons that we have learned on the ground, and to guide them toward more effective approaches. Organizations must create their own space to build successful models and then have the discipline to reject funding that compromises their programs. As nonprofits, our work must be driven by our missions, not our donations.

Marissa Sackler is the founder of Beespace, a nonprofit incubator based in New York that provides its grantees with office space and operational support, as well as mentorship relationships with established leaders in both the nonprofit and other fields. She is a founding sponsor and activist for Charity: Water, serves on the board of trustees for the Dia Art Foundation, and is a member of the advisory boards for Invisible Children, Last Mile Health, and Global Citizen's Global Poverty Project. She is also an accomplished photographer, focusing on documenting social injustice.

Let's begin by talking about 20 percent, the industry standard for non-profits' overhead costs. Where did this come from?

SACKLER: I don't think that anybody actually knows why 20 percent has become the industry standard for nonprofits' overhead costs; it's just a number that we all seem to knowingly toss around. Yet there is no empirical evidence that organizations function more effectively if they spend 20 percent on overhead costs or 40 percent on overhead costs.

Lack of evidence aside, is this a reasonable expectation? Can nonprofits be effective while spending no more than 20 percent of their budgets on overhead?

SACKLER: Well, for starters, different organizations require different types of overhead, so the idea that there is a universal percentage that all nonprofits should aim to reach is absurd. Handing out packets of protein paste, for instance, requires very little overhead spending, compared to programs that provide intensive agricultural interventions to reduce pervasive food security. Yet both generate important, albeit different, impacts. So how can we hold both organizations to the same standards?

This expectation is also detrimental to nonprofits, many of which cannot operate on just 20 percent of their income or less. Some will forgo technological upgrades, staff development initiatives, and expansion simply because they don't want their overhead to rise above this magic number. Yet, without these investments, their impact is limited. They cannot grow. They cannot innovate. How could we expect them to? I've seen nonprofits cram fifteen people into hallways to take their meetings, all because they didn't want to spend money on a bigger office space. Still others invent creative accounting that diverts traditional overhead costs into their programs budget. Almost every

(continued)

organization that I have worked with plays this game. They have to. But this practice undermines transparency and accountability.

How can nonprofits be more honest with their funders? What responsibility do they have in shifting this "overhead myth"?

SACKLER: That's a tough question. I think that nonprofits and donors do need to have more honest conversations, and I also believe that organizations have a responsibility to inform funders. It's not beneficial for anyone to be dishonest. Yet, if their supporters do not trust their expertise or their knowledge, it's difficult for many nonprofits to be forthright. They simply do not have enough funding to lose donors. So I think we have to look toward larger nonprofits that have substantial enough budgets to lead the conversation. Organizations that have higher overhead costs but continue to drive significant changes must speak up; smaller, more grassroots institutions can follow. Nonprofits must also stop touting low overhead percentages as indicators of success. They play a role in this dysfunctional dynamic as well.

Do organizations have a standard definition of overhead? Should we?

SACKLER: I certainly think that, even if we do not necessarily have a standardized definition of overhead, we should at least differentiate between good and bad overhead costs. I won't deny that frivolous spending does occur in the nonprofit industry. I am just saying that it shouldn't fall under the same definition as infrastructure upgrades or more effective recruitment strategy investments. The two are fundamentally different types of "overhead."

Moving away from this 20 percent overhead benchmark, what should philanthropists consider when investing in nonprofits?

SACKLER: Impact. Think about it: When we invest in a corporation, we focus almost solely on the return on our investments. Most of us do not care about what the company had to do to increase our profit margins. Shouldn't we apply that same standard of thinking to the nonprofit sector? Many donors have become so focused on overhead that they have forgotten about organizations' impact. I think that we need to refocus philanthropists' attention on nonprofits' performance. If an organization is driving sustainable, lasting change in disadvantaged communities, funders should seek to empower them. Instead of asking fund-raising questions, they should ask about what the program needs to expand either vertically or horizontally.

CHAPTER EIGHT

Taking the Stage

IN LATE 2006, A DELEGATION FROM THE CLINTON GLOBAL INITIATIVE arrived at our offices. They were looking for a child-headed household—a family in which both the parents had died, and one sibling was taking care of younger ones. One afternoon, we gathered forty clients in our courtyard to talk about their experiences. In typical fashion, Zethu stole the show. She spoke articulately about the challenges of being both a mother and a sister to Star and Lungi, all while flashing her million-watt smile. Her charm can be difficult to resist. It was clear that she was the one they would choose to represent Ubuntu, and soon she'd garnered an invitation to address the midyear meeting of the Clinton Global Initiative in New York City.

We'd become a Clinton Global Initiative commitment site in 2006, with Vincent and Anne Mai's pledge of support for our programs for orphaned and vulnerable children. (The Clinton Global Initiative challenges organizations and individuals to come up with new, specific, and measurable approaches to significant challenges; CGI's goal is to foster innovation, rather than to implement programs themselves.) Vincent and Anne had always been deeply committed donors, and we'd developed a strong relationship. They were willing to take a chance on us because they understood our mission and they trusted our knowledge of the townships. For example, when I approached them about sponsoring health insurance for all our employees—something we felt strongly about, but didn't have the operating budget to provide—they immediately pledged their support. They were glad to see Ubuntu, and Zethu, get the spotlight at the midyear meeting.

Zethu and Fezeka traveled to New York in April of 2007. It was the first time Zethu had left Eastern Cape province, and even boarding the plane was exhilarating. "I think that was my first break of experiencing good things in life, having to fly in an airplane for the first time. Just being in the plane itself felt very special," she told me. "It gave me the feeling that good things are not attached to specific people."

Before Zethu took the stage, we sat together in the green room along with President Clinton, the CEO of Time Warner, and the actor Kevin Spacey. I felt overwhelmed by the star power. It was one of the only occasions in my adult life when I have felt compelled to wear a tie; amazingly, President Clinton did say to me, "Jacob, that's a nice tie you're wearing."

Waiting there, I was so tense that I could barely function. I leaned over to Zethu and said, "Does it make you nervous to be around all these people?"

She retorted, "I'm not nervous, I don't know who any of these people are." And when she went up to speak, she was calm and confident.

In a few stark words, she told the room how she came to be the primary caregiver for her siblings. "I lost my father in 2004 and my mother died in 2005, because of HIV and AIDS. It was too hard for me, I couldn't face it. I started asking myself some questions. Questions like *What am I supposed to do? Should I go? Should I just run away? I've got dreams. I don't know what can do this to me. How can I face this thing?* But I told myself, *These are my siblings. This is my sister, this is my brother. I love them. They deserve the best. So, what can stop me? I have to do this.* But it was really, really hard."

She described going to the Ubuntu counselor in her school, who introduced her to Fezeka. "Sis* Fezeka Mzalazala saw me and my siblings staying in a small shack room with eight people, staying with our aunt," she recalled. "And unfortunately, my aunt was not able to take care of all of us. She left to Johannesburg. She left us with no home and no hope. Sis Fezeka Mzalazala worked so hard in order for us to get a safe place, just as every child."

She described all the things Ubuntu had provided for her family—food, electricity, school fees, and uniforms. "When I grow up, I would like to be a chartered accountant," she went on. "But I wasn't doing well in mathematics. But Ubuntu tutored me in their afternoon program that they have in my school." Zethu added with a laugh, "Now I live and breathe with mathematics."

She noted, "Each and every home has a father and a mother who is a breadwinner. But in my family, Ubuntu is my breadwinner, because of everything that Ubuntu has done for me."

Finally, she thanked the Clinton Global Initiative and the Mais and concluded, "I believe that a commitment is a promise. I'm standing here as a child from South Africa. I believe that I can change the world. My commitment is that when I get back to South Africa, I could start a support group for orphan girls in my school. This is my way of changing the world."

As the audience rose in a standing ovation, President Clinton wrapped her in a hug. As he took the podium, he quipped, "Before you become an accountant, I think you should seriously consider politics. I might even become a citizen in South Africa to vote for you."

---

* A South African term of respect.

~~~~~~~~

While we were in New York, Zethu had many incredible experiences. Not only was she treated like a rock star by the former president of the United States, but she also ate herself sick at every meal, went on a shopping spree at FAO Schwartz, and was interviewed by a New York morning TV show. Every day, she was showered with praise, attention, and affection. By the end of the week, her head had been turned, and her ego had been greatly inflated. To then go back to ordinary life, back to being a student and a parent, was understandably difficult.

And then, she also came back to great media interest. She'd thought that no one in South Africa would even know about her speech, and Ubuntu, naively, didn't brace her at all for the attention. Worst of all, we hadn't prepared her for the fact that her parents' status would now be public. "It was very overwhelming, it was too much pressure for me," Zethu remembers. "I was like, *Okay, Jake didn't tell me that, he didn't tell me that the HIV status of my parents is going to be out, just like that, in the newspapers and magazines, that teachers at school—everyone is going to know.* It was just a nightmare."

It didn't happen right away, but slowly Zethu fell off track. She started to dress more provocatively, to go out with friends at night instead of studying, and generally acted like a rebellious teen. She stopped showing up for her commitments at Ubuntu, and her grades began to slip. We did what any parent would do in that situation: We kept reaching out to her, but we also made it clear that we had expectations for her.

Throughout this period, Fezeka continued to check in with Zethu and her family, even as Zethu often resisted her overtures. "Zethu used to laugh at me because as I saw her growing and becoming a teenager, I started to wear my hat of becoming a mother," Fezeka remembers. "I was starting to ask her about boyfriends, is she on family planning, is she tested, if she has a boyfriend, has she slept with the boyfriend. At that point she looked at me, and she was scared at first to talk to me about those things. So I started to develop that relationship with her. She can start to feel comfortable to talk about those things so she can be safe and not be infected with HIV or get pregnant."

Finally, after about four months of bad behavior, Zethu showed up again at Ubuntu, looking like the old Zethu: wearing more suitable clothes, smiling, ready to work her way back. Qondakele had called her and had a blunt conversation with her about what she was doing with her life. "He said, 'I don't like A, B, C, and D about you, I think you can sort this and this and that, and then you can actually come back,'" she recalled. "That turned me around." It made her stop and consider the consequences of her actions. She remembers, "I came to a point where I thought, *No, man, I need to be mature, be a lady, and start to dream big about my future.*"

<hr>

With more visibility from conferences like the Clinton Global Initiative, the World Economic Forum, and being recognized with a fellowship from the Aspen Institute, we started to get more donors, more media attention, and more celebrity backers. I've never gotten used to the dissonance this sort of thing created. I'd be in Port Elizabeth in the morning, talking to our clients, children who had been raped, orphaned, abandoned. Then I'd get on a plane, and when I landed, my first job would be to call Chuck D to see if he'd help us out at an event, or to go to lunch with Donna Karan.

One of the most surreal moments happened around our ten-year anniversary gala, in 2009. Kyra Sedgwick and Kevin Bacon had been involved for some time, and Kevin and I met one day for lunch to talk about his role emceeing the gala. It was clear that a couple near us was looking at us and whispering; it was hard for me not to feel self-conscious, though Kevin didn't seem to notice. As we got up to leave, the couple said, "Excuse us for a moment?" He turned, ready to take a photo or sign an autograph, while I started to walk away, a little embarrassed.

And then the man said, "Wait—are you Jacob Lief?" Kevin loved it. It turned out that the guy had worked with my father twenty years earlier. "You look just like him," he told me.

As we walked out, Kevin shook his head and said, "Wow, that's a first."

Meanwhile, Lungi was becoming a star in her own right. She and Zethu shared a vivacious charm, intelligence, and eloquence. She'd so impressed one of our board members that he sponsored her to enroll at the Diocesan School for Girls (DSG) in Grahamstown—one of the best boarding schools in the region, with students from some of the most prestigious families on the continent. She wasn't entirely prepared for it; how could she be? The other girls had gone to private school all their lives; even with the tutoring Ubuntu provided, Lungi started at a disadvantage.

I took her up to the school, along with Qondakele. After we arrived, the house lady approached me and asked that I take Lungi shopping for a bra, because she was clearly developing and didn't have anything. I told Lungi we were going to go get some clothes. We went into a department store and we walked around, kind of aimlessly. I couldn't think of how to broach the subject with her. Finally, I saw an older woman outside who looked nice, and I said, "Listen, mama, this is my student. She needs to get a bra. Will you take this money and go in there?" The woman looked at me and laughed, and agreed. Still chuckling, she took Lungi by the arm and led her to the underwear department.

Fezeka traveled up to the school a few days later to finish getting Lungi prepared for the year. Now that Lungi had seen the difference in the girls she was going to be living with, her expectations had begun to exceed her means. Lungi and Fezeka went to the school shop to pick out a uniform; the shop had both new ones and ones that were used, but still practically new. When they got to the shop, Lungi told Fezeka, "No way, I don't want an old uniform, I want a new one."

Fezeka shook her head and said, "Here's what we are going to do. We are going to buy two uniforms, one old, and the second one new." And, she went on, the uniforms were going to be long, so she didn't need to buy new ones each year. "I'm sure she was not happy about it," Fezeka recalls. "But I took a decision as a parent at that time, and we agreed to that."

Looking back, I feel that we set Lungi up to fail. She wasn't prepared, and though we did everything we could to make sure she would have academic and social support there, we were two hours away. She was dealing with culture shock and academic shock, and it was no surprise that after her first year she was condoned: She could go back, but only if she repeated the same year.

Still, she talked about the school with enthusiasm. At our tenth anniversary gala in New York City, she was a featured speaker. Kevin Bacon introduced her. "It's hard to describe the energy that you feel coming off of this child," he said. "She's absolutely beautiful and sparkles with a kind of very inspirational light." She wore her DSG uniform, and the thing I remember most about her speech is how small and vulnerable she looked there onstage, in front of five hundred people, and yet how strong and vibrant she was as she spoke. She didn't just invite the audience's attention—she commanded it.

She described her feelings when her mother died, when she was nine. "My mother went to the hospital one night and never came back. And that was the saddest night of my whole, whole life." And she spoke about the dedication of Zethu, and the warmth of Fezeka, and the way that Ubuntu had filled, as much as we could, the void that the loss of her parents had left. And then she talked about what she was doing now. "Last year, I was enrolled in DSG, a school that is known for academic excellence. It's a great school, and it's an opportunity I never thought I would have. I'm safe, I'm empowered, I'm a dancer, I'm an actor. And all of these things are because of Ubuntu."

She stayed in New York with Andrew Rolfe, a South African ex-pat whom I'd met through Vincent Mai. He had joined our board and immediately began making a huge difference in building our company. With his background in private equity, he was able to bring valuable knowledge about structure and management. But he also had a strong personal connection to South Africa. He and his family adored Lungi, and they were thrilled to have her in their Park Avenue apartment for a week. When I dropped her off there, her eyes widened and she seemed afraid to blink, for fear it might all disappear—this beautiful apartment with its spacious, comfortable rooms. Andrew remembers how bubbly and bright and confident she was during that visit, but also that they got to see the other side of her—the little girl without a mother. Andrew's wife, Fabiola, had long conversations with her deep into the night.

Unfortunately, Lungi wasn't able pull herself out of the academic rut she'd gotten into. Even when repeating the same grade, she failed dismally. Fezeka, Jana, Gcobani, and I met to discuss the situation and assess our options. Should we see if she could take extra classes and try again? We decided we needed to find another school, one in Port Elizabeth, one where she actually had the opportunity to succeed. We knew it would be difficult for Lungi, because after being enrolled in this stellar school, after spending two years with girls who saw no limits on their allowance, after being in New York and living on Park Avenue and rubbing shoulders with Kevin Bacon, she saw herself as better than the other kids in the township. Coming back would not be easy.

<hr />

Star, the middle child between Zethu and Lungi, sometimes seemed overpowered by the sheer wattage of his sisters. He was a sweet, respectful boy, but, as Zethu and Fezeka recall, as the years went on it became clear that he suffered deeply from the loss of his parents. Star never did very well in school, or seemed to care much about his studies. And as he entered his teenage years, he became paranoid. He stopped going to classes, and when Fezeka asked him why, he told her that he felt like he smelled. She said, "I'm sitting with you now, and I'm not smelling anything. You're washed, you have a clean uniform, Zethu is washing your clothes. Why do you feel like there's a smell?" He told her that he heard people laughing at him, and that he couldn't go back to school.

It soon became apparent to those around him that he suffered from psychological problems. One night, he became very angry for no clear reason and locked Zethu and Lungi out of the apartment. The girls were scared of what he might do to the apartment, to himself, or to them. "That's the day that I said, you know, this one has a problem," Zethu remembers. "There is trouble." They called Fezeka, who was able to calm Star down and get him to open the door.

But his condition continued to deteriorate. One afternoon, Fezeka got a call that Star had been found on New Brighton Beach. He'd been walking around the beach for hours, swaddled in a heavy blanket even though it was a hot summer day. Others on the beach, worried he was going to kill himself, called the police. They brought him to Ubuntu, and Fezeka began the difficult task of finding a safe place for him to stay. It was Friday night, and the social worker at the closest group home for teens in trouble told Fezeka there was no way to take Star in without papers from the Department of Social Development. Finally, Fezeka convinced him to take in Star until Monday, when she could bring the proper documents.

Of course, nothing runs that easily in a bureaucracy. Fezeka went to Social Development; they sent her to the police station. At the police station, they sent her to the juvenile courts. At the courts, the magistrate for juveniles was on leave. They sent her to a court social worker, who listened to her story and then asked, "Where does he stay?" When Fezeka told them Kwazakhele, the social worker told her, "No, we don't work in that area. You have to see Social Development." Back to Social Development. Yet again, they sent her away to see the woman in charge of crisis cases. Fezeka waited outside her office until the end of the day, but the woman never showed up.

Fezeka called the group home to ask them not to kick Star out, that she was working with the department to get the paperwork. She never succeeded, but her continuing efforts and her dedication to visiting Star impressed the social workers at the home. "They could see that I was part of the process," Fezeka remembers. Star stayed at the juvenile home, where he was kept safe and well fed for two years, until he was eighteen.

<center>~~~~~~</center>

In 2007, we saw our first nineteen students begin university, all of them on scholarships provided by Ubuntu. None of these young men and women—including Sipho, Nozibele, and Lwando from our Young Ambassadors Program—had had any thoughts of attaining an education beyond high school. But here they were, about to start a whole new phase of their lives, one that no one in their families had ever experienced before.

Qondakele oversaw much of this initiative, which was joyful and exciting for all of us, but also a challenge to manage.

"Our scholarship for university is on a case-by-case basis, I can't tell you how much it is, I can't tell you how much it is going to cost," Qondakele noted. "If I send my daughter to university, I'm going to buy her what she needs. It's not just tuition and room and board, it's books. If she needs underwear, I'm going to buy her underwear. And I'd rather say that the future of Ubuntu is raising kids."

In South Africa, you start determining your career by the time you are fifteen. Students are given points based on their achievement in each subject. You have to hit the right points in order to qualify for the university course you want, and if you don't get those points, there's no starting over. So it was essential to work with the students to find the proper course of study, to determine the right schools to apply to, and to make sure that we were putting them on a pathway to success, not failure.

Equally important was that we needed to make sure our staff members could make decisions and guide their clients with their heads, not their hearts. Often, a staff member works with a student from early childhood into their teenage years; they feel a deep connection to them that often feels like a familial bond (and, in some cases, a client is part of a staff member's extended family). These personal feelings can impact one's judgment, but we're not doing any student a favor by setting her on course to become an engineer if she doesn't have the aptitude for engineering.

The evolution of the program created some tension. A few years ago, Jana began to take over its supervision, and together she and Qondakele gave the students—known as the Ubuntu Scholars—a talk they called "Entitlement versus Integrity." We'd seen students taking our support for granted over the years, doing five or six years of schooling as they changed their minds about courses and majors. We let them know that they needed to be accountable for their performance and seriousness of purpose, and that no one was entitled to a scholarship.

The room felt filled with negativity, Jana remembers, and she left thinking that their speech had had little impact on these students. But not long ago, she had another meeting with scholarship recipients. One boy in particular had done very well in the past year, and she asked him what had inspired him. He told her, "Jana, do you remember that speech you and Qondakele gave about entitlement and integrity?"

At times, students who seem most a part of Ubuntu fall away. During a shift in the way we administered the scholarships, we asked all our students to apply first for the national financial aid scheme, and then to come talk to us about what further support they might need. A student named Sina, who was one of our most brilliant students and enrolled at Rhodes University, failed to get any financial aid. She'd been with us for several years, and often spoke to donors and to other students about Ubuntu. Though we'd said many times that we would continue to support students who didn't get financial aid through the government, that we wouldn't leave anyone completely without funding, she started to say that Ubuntu had decided not to pay her tuition. She was through with us.

Jana called and e-mailed her many times, letting her know that she only needed to apply for our scholarship and we would work it out. Sina never responded. She managed to find funding herself, and continued at Rhodes. Luckily, she's a young woman with the ability and the resources to find her own course, but too often in these situations, the end result is not so positive. We work in a complicated environment; students leave our programs for many reasons, from mental illness to disinterest to pride, and not everyone who leaves Ubuntu will fail, just as not everyone who sticks with us will succeed. Ubuntu steadfastly remains a resource for all these young men and women, whenever they want it, and whenever they feel ready to meet the requirements we set for them. No matter what, they are our family, and we'll embrace them.

Despite some setbacks, the Ubuntu Scholars program has seen great successes over the years. Nearly fifty of our students have graduated from university. Our young men and women have attended schools from Nelson Mandela Metropolitan University in Port Elizabeth to the University of Cape Town and Rhodes University to Hult International Business School in London. One of our scholars, Maputi, started attending Ubuntu programs in 2002. She reminisced, "I recall receiving a LIBRARY MONITOR badge at an Ubuntu Education Fund event coupled by my first three storybooks. I can still remember the titles of the books, which were *Max Bonker and the Howling Thieves, Best Beak in Boonaroo Bay,* and *Noah's Ark.*" In 2014, she graduated from West Virginia University with a degree in biometric engineering.

～～～～～

For several years, our chairman (following Tom Jaffe) had been Daniel Osorio, who now heads a hedge fund focusing on Latin America. His younger brother, Santiago, had been a classmate and close friend of mine in London. Daniel has incredible charisma, and he was able to see the risky moves we needed to make, to understand the thinking behind them, and to sell those decisions to the rest of the board—to accept

PEPFAR funding, for instance, and to leave the schools. (Another board member who supported us throughout was Rush McCloy, our financial chair and an incredible mentor to Tarryn and me. At one point, he was serving in Afghanistan as a navy reserve officer while also running his own fund, and yet he'd still respond to our requests for advice.)

In late 2006, I took another bold idea to Daniel. We wanted to construct a new building for Ubuntu, one that could house our staff, our programs, and give us room to accommodate our ambitions to do more for the community. We wanted our own pediatric clinic to provide health services; a pharmacy to dispense medicine; room for an industrial kitchen, for choir practice, for counseling and tutoring. At the same time, our community needed a visible reminder that they deserved the most beautiful, most state-of-the-art building we could dream up, something that children in Manhattan or London might have access to.

It was something that Banks and I had talked about since we started Ubuntu: Wouldn't it be great to have a real center, room to grow, windows, more than one bathroom? Everyone told us it wasn't possible. We had an excellent fund-raising operation, but would we be able to raise enough? We asked some of New York's top nonprofit consultants how we should go about structuring a capital campaign for six to seven million dollars on top of bringing in enough money for our operating budget. Every one told us that we weren't ready, that we would cannibalize our annual fund-raising and ultimately destroy Ubuntu.

We also often heard the warning "This is going to change your goals, your mission." No, it's not. What we do is get these kids from point A to point B. This is going to help us get there. Our kids can't get the health care they need? Let's build our own clinic. They're not getting a good enough education? Let's build our own school. There's no place to do after-school theater? Let's do that. We were serving five hundred meals a day out of a shipping container—let's build an industrial kitchen. Nothing embodies our philosophy and who we are better than the Ubuntu Centre: It's about excellence, focus, investment, about having everything right there.

And after many conversations about the purpose of the Ubuntu Centre, Daniel knew what we needed to do. As chairman, Daniel gave me unwavering support and encouraged me to be big and bold. At the time, that's exactly what we needed: to ignore conservative advice and go forward, full steam ahead. He helped us convince the rest of the board that taking risks had made Ubuntu take shape in the first place, and that every risk we took made us stronger as an organization. And so we made the decision that we'd begin our capital campaign for the Ubuntu Centre.

Our next chairman, Andrew Rolfe, who had hosted Lungi during the gala, brought equally valuable tools to Ubuntu. Our board had long been focused on fund-raising and moral support, which was what we had needed for many years. But Andrew saw that Ubuntu needed a board that also could guide us in governance and strategy rather than in just pure fund-raising. Andrew also made sure to take me aside and say, "How can we make this job livable for you?" He added, "I'm going to focus on you, Jake." No one had ever said that to me before, and it turned out to make a huge difference for all of us. By taking care of me, Andrew allowed me to take care of others.

At the time, I'd started to ponder leaving Ubuntu. I wasn't enjoying myself and often felt on the verge of a nervous breakdown. The loneliness of my position had begun to overwhelm me. As the face of Ubuntu, the person out soliciting donations, making sure that we had enough money to meet all our operating expenses, the pressure was intense. I not only bore the burden of all the fears and concerns of our leadership team, but also felt directly responsible for the livelihoods of dozens of other people. We had a very slim cash cushion, so there was no room for error. And I always knew that if I walked away, Ubuntu wouldn't survive. As the organization became larger, it became more difficult to feel like I was just one of the team. Because of my position, even the simplest off-the-cuff remark to someone in the hallway suddenly meant more than I had intended.

The whole leadership team was feeling pressures of their own, which came with long hours and emotionally wearing work. We were growing as an organization and becoming a special kind of hybrid: We were still grassroots in that we were based in the community and worked closely with and responded swiftly to our community, but we took a more systematized, professional approach than your typical grassroots. But our structure at the top hadn't caught up, and we were all filling too many roles and finding our lines of communication too often crossed.

The truth is that we had been working at a start-up pace—twelve-plus hours a day, six or sometimes seven days a week—for eight years. But unlike a tech start-up, there was no buyout in the works. None of us were going to become millionaires overnight from an IPO, and none of us expected to, but we all longed for some stability in our lives. Lindsay and I were now married and thinking about children; Jordan and Jana, too, now married, wanted to start a family. By this time, both Banks and Gcobani had left their teaching positions to devote themselves to Ubuntu, at a financial cost to themselves. Gcobani had two sons who would be starting university shortly, and both he and Banks worried about whether their children would be taken care of in the future, without the security of the government pension their teaching jobs would have provided. Qondakele also had children to think about, and he had ambitions of his own that might not ultimately find satisfaction at Ubuntu. Tarryn had the skill and the drive to get a job anywhere she liked for a much larger salary, but all she wanted was to get the title of CFO, which she felt would validate her long hours.

What Andrew could see was that restructuring the organization would relieve a great deal of that pressure. It's something he did all the time in his job: Take companies and build systems to make them successful. He'd done it with Pret A Manger, with Gap, and with Jimmy Choo.

Andrew's method often involved asking me pointed questions that challenged me to implement solutions. One of the first ones he asked was "If you got an extra one million dollars, where would you spend it?" That pushed us to invest in a cost breakdown analysis so we could establish a four-year financial plan. Later, Scott Shleifer, an old college acquaintance who worked in the financial world, approached me about joining our board.

He told me, "I believe in you, but you can't translate your work in the way I'd like to see. Let me hire McKinsey"—the management consulting firm—"for you, and if their report looks good, I'll make a commitment." The process of being audited by McKinsey helped us build a system to collect and make sense of data, to better measure Ubuntu's economic impact, and to translate that impact in a way that made sense to a broader audience.

As our financial picture began to become clearer, Andrew also helped me get the senior leadership into better-defined, more-structured positions. We created distinctions in roles and responsibilities that had never existed before: Who approves which expenditures? Who deals with hiring and firing decisions? Everyone had always done a little bit of everything, but once each one of us had a specific role and could let go of some of the other functions, it became easier to get things done, and less stressful.

The most dramatic shift in the leadership structure may have been taking Banks from a day-to-day role to a more broad-minded leadership position with the title of senior advisor. Part of me wanted to call the position chief *ubuntu* officer, because in many ways that's what Banks does so well: He makes people feel respected and empowered, and he has always been an important link to our community. There would be no Ubuntu without Banks. But at the same time, he wasn't happy trying to fill the role of CEO in a company with eighty employees; that role didn't make sense for him.

Tarryn became chief financial officer, managing finance, administration, and HR; Jana became the chief programs officer, supervising household stability, health, and educational interventions; and Jordan took on the role of chief external relations officer, overseeing marketing and communications, special events, and grants. Qondakele became the director of our South Africa External Relations Department. (A few years later, Qondakele left Ubuntu for an impressive position in the development department at Rhodes University.) All reported to me. Gcobani, as deputy president, remained active in strategic decisions as well as community outreach, and served as the face of fund-raising in South Africa. Suddenly, we all had mandates, we all knew what our targets were, what we needed to accomplish, and what we had authority over.

Andrew's approach was respectful and collaborative. From day one, Andrew told me, "Jake, you know your business. I'm not going to tell you how to run it. I can give you advice and knowledge, but only you can make these decisions." At times, I resisted; when he brought up Jimmy Choo, I thought it was ridiculous to compare high-end women's shoes to vulnerable children. But he showed me that the same basic business practices applied: develop a middle management structure, create systems and enhance accountability, and allow the senior leadership to focus on the long-term strategic goals. The greatest thing Andrew gave me was his time. We had long conversations regularly, and we talked about everything from Ubuntu to family to religion. I finally felt like I had someone to lean on, and my position wasn't so lonely anymore.

CHANGING THE CONVERSATION: STARTING EARLY

IN MUCH OF the world, parenting only begins with the birth of the child. Although we know that choices that are made during pregnancy have implications well into childhood and beyond, mothers all too often lack access to prenatal care. In the townships of South Africa, women go through the entire pregnancy without ever seeing their growing child on an ultrasound—a standard procedure for women in the United States. For a pregnant mother with HIV, getting early and excellent care is vital for her own health and that of her child.

Once that child is born, malnutrition, parental illiteracy, and a range of additional poverty-related factors can have lasting, irreversible developmental consequences. Children attain significant physical, cognitive, and social developmental milestones during the first five years of their lives. Brain growth, for instance, is at its highest from birth to age three, forming processes that have lasting effects on a child's cognitive capacities. This period is also critical because of the dramatic changes in sensory, motor, and language capabilities that occur.

Over and over again, we saw what happened without early intervention: A typical grade-ten high school student, even if she'd been working with Ubuntu since elementary school, scored at a grade-seven level on assessment tests in math and English. And as we looked more deeply, we found these gaps existed as early as three years of age. We were providing intensive tutoring, after-school programs, summer camps, yet we could not bridge the differences in achievement. Their roots were in the earliest years of these children's lives.

So now, at Ubuntu, interventions begin when a woman becomes pregnant. We offer ultrasounds, nutrition programs, and prevention of mother-to-child-transmission services for mothers with HIV. Following a healthy birth, parents are enrolled in workshops for the first months of their child's life and given support and household stability services to make sure their home is safe.

Support continues into a world-class early-childhood education program, with holistic services integrated into the classroom—from immunizations and other clinical services to home visits and stability interventions to more parenting workshops. We are determined to give the children we work with every advantage, and that means we want to give them the best care, even before they are born.

Tovah Klein, PhD, is an associate professor of psychology at Barnard College and the director of the Barnard College Center for Toddler Development. She and her team of researchers look at the social and emotional development of children, the effect on parents of raising a toddler, and the interplay between child and parent. Klein also acts as a developmental advisor to Sesame Street, serves on the advisory boards of Room to Grow and Rwanda Education Assistance Project and is the author of *How Toddlers Thrive: What Parents Can Do Today for Children Ages 2–5 to Plant the Seeds of Lifelong Success.* Klein also sits on the advisory board for Ubuntu Education Fund.

Why has it taken so long for this philanthropic community to embrace the idea of "starting early"?

KLEIN: Back in the 1960s, we didn't think that babies could even see at birth. There was a real sense that young children were blank slates unaware of their surroundings. It's taken us a very long time to shift the general public's perspective and convince people that babies are not passive "sponges," but rather they are active agents. I think that, personally, it is disrespectful to children to not recognize them as active change agents.

The other missing piece in this discussion is our failure to realize the value of relationships. What's the heart of a good beginning for any child anywhere in the world? It's a loving, nurturing relationship. It doesn't have to be a mother or a father; it can be with a grandparent, aunt, or uncle. Children just have to have someone who meets their needs, loves them, and responds to them in a caring way. If children do not have that support system to deal with their emotional stability, then the future of their development is really in jeopardy.

The irony in all of this is that Head Start actually began in the sixties and really was a hallmark of the "starting early" philosophy. I think that it has just taken a long time to debunk misconceptions about children, their development, and the importance of relationships in their lives. I think that once society really moves past this idea of babies and children as passive, the philanthropic community will better understand the need for earlier interventions. Babies are learning in utero and from the moment they enter this world. Give them good, nurturing relationships and inputs, and they will thrive. Feed them bad stuff, and the brain will take that in instead.

(continued)

What happens to the children who need but do not receive those early investments?

KLEIN: Children who grow up in stressful homes without nurturing, loving relationships will likely experience developmental delays. They also will grow up not believing in themselves and not learning to trust that adults can help them. Everyday stressors can have a significant impact on children's futures— almost like a small drip that continues to get worse with time. Worries like financial instability, food insecurity, and neighborhood violence constantly stress families and undermine parents' ability to provide their children with a solid foundation at home. Children need this stability during the first five years of life; it allows them to develop resilience so that, later on in life, they can manage adversities on their own and bounce back.

We now have neuroscience and developmental psychology data that show what happens to children when they do not receive early interventions. They show that, during the first two to five years of life, there is tremendous brain growth, with many neural connections being formed. This becomes the foundation that later development is built upon. So the question is, can interventions be successful with a child who has never known a nurturing relationship or whose brain has been deprived of basic nutrients? If children's development is delayed in this critical period, we can still intervene later on in life, but progress will be far more costly and come more slowly. There may also be some gaps that we just won't be able to fill in.

Just how powerful can "starting early" be in a child's life? How can we convince philanthropists to invest in childhood development?

KLEIN: That's something that I grapple with all the time. It's hard for me to not get past the basic human decency argument—that all children deserve to receive the same level of support and caring relationships and to have access to opportunities so they can thrive. But we can also point to more than fifty years of data that show the effects of early interventions. Children enrolled in high-quality early-childhood programs show much better outcomes as adults— higher educational attainment and salary earnings, lower rates of incarceration, and better physical and mental health. We know that early support pays off over the lifetime.

Tell me more about the toddler center at Barnard.

KLEIN: At the toddler center, we begin working with children who are eighteen months old. At that age, children are just starting to become their own person, and they need an emotionally safe environment to explore and figure out who they are and how the world works. In a classroom setting, we provide space for children to be curious, active agents that can engage with toys, art materials, etc. They slowly develop the notion that "adults will still take care of me," and this understanding empowers them to navigate their world on their own.

So what would you say are the absolute most important things that you can do to stabilize a toddler's environment?

KLEIN: One of the most important things that we can provide is both physical and psychological safety. Toddlers need to know not only that they are safe from physical harm and violence, but that they are also secure in their relationships. They need to feel that their nurturing support systems will always be there for them regardless of what happens.

After establishing this secure environment by building trusting relationships between the child and the teachers, we foster an engaging space where children feel that they can explore their worlds through play. There are materials in our room that support their learning—books, climbing toys, sand and Play-Doh for exploration, art materials, and pretend play. As the young children try out new materials and objects, they figure out "Hey, I can do this!" which gives them confidence and a sense of agency. This is how the love of learning develops, with that sense of pride, of being able to figure things out for themselves. This is also where being independent starts—with doing things for themselves. But always with the support of adults, especially in times of need like comfort or working out frustrations, anger, and other hard feelings they encounter along the way.

CHAPTER NINE

A Building with Wings

THE FIRST STEP TO BUILDING THE UBUNTU CENTRE WAS, LIKE ALL OF OUR other initiatives, to get buy-in from the community. We spent two months talking to people about the building, what it might look like, what we'd do there, and how much it would cost. Banks remembers one granny saying to him, "It's too much money. Why don't you give us bread and soup instead, to fill our stomachs?"

He told her, "I'm here now, and I can give that to you. But this building will be here forever, and it will always be yours."

"That can't be done here, that's something for town," other people would tell us. There's a mentality that if you want something nice, you "build it in town"—the predominantly white, wealthy areas. For too many projects in poor communities, the more money you have, the bigger a box you build. There's no thought to beauty, to inspiration. But the role that architecture plays is profound. The Ubuntu Centre was made for us, for our use, and it was built to represent the potential of our community. The psychological impact that makes shouldn't be downplayed.

Over time, we convinced people that this made sense for the community, and for our organization. Early on, we realized that as part of our buy-in, we needed to launch our capital campaign in the township. Every board member and every staff member made a pledge. And the first 222,000 rand—a little more than $20,000—of the $7 million we'd eventually raise came from community members. A mama would pull two rand (about twenty cents) out of her bra and put it in our donation bucket, along with a slip of paper with her name on it. Once the building went up, we promised, there would be a wall with every donor's name in alphabetical order—whether the donation was two rand or a million dollars.

A separate challenge was convincing donors outside of the community to invest in the project. In some ways, the challenge resembled what we faced in the townships—convincing people that a building like this belonged in our community. People had become enamored with the idea of using shipping containers for low-cost building: They're cheap, they're utilitarian, they can be repurposed in lots of useful ways. Ubuntu has used its fair share. But in the summer, they're boiling hot, and in the winter, they're freezing. At the end of the day, no matter how you paint it or reconfigure it, it's a shipping container. But this model of building reflects a mind-set that when you are working in the context of poverty, it is somehow immoral to dream of providing something of the same quality that you'd find in any wealthy enclave.

At one fund-raising talk, I lost my patience with this line of questioning. I was on the Upper West Side of Manhattan, talking about the Ubuntu Centre. Someone asked how we defined it, and I answered that it was an extension of everything that we do, in a better setting and with greater resources. I mentioned the six to seven million-dollar budget, and a woman in the audience spoke up. "I don't understand how you can justify spending this much money in such poverty," she said. "You could feed the whole city for that much money."

I believe that you shouldn't have to be born on the Upper West Side to have access to beauty and quality. It's common sense that you want to put your children in the best possible environment, with the best possible opportunities. I asked her if she had children, and when she said yes, I asked her where they went to school. It was Dalton, a school that costs $40,000 a year, had not long before completed a $50 million capital campaign, and has a top-notch integrated technology education program. I don't understand how it is fine to provide your own children with the best resources, but to deny those resources to someone else's child. So I said, "Your children's school just did a huge capital campaign. Why don't our kids deserve the same thing?"

Most people would say yes, access to education and health services for children is vital. But as soon as you start to address the quality of that access, people aren't as quick to agree. When it is someone else's child, it's easier to think about cost cutting.

At the same time, having a tangible goal—a building made of concrete and glass that would rise in the townships, with specific costs for materials and labor—made it easier in many ways for people to give money. When I told someone, "We're building a community center," she could think of the place where she had gone for summer camp as a child. Or if I told another person, "It's going to have a theater," he could think of the play he went to the other day. Telling someone that his money was going to HIV/AIDS education—that's not so easy to picture. It's akin to the Sally Struthers syndrome: People like to know how many children they are saving with each donation, even if it doesn't work that way. It makes them feel connected.

And we found a receptive audience at many of our fund-raising meetings. We received a lead gift from Stan and Fiona Druckenmiller. Another came from the Tabatznik family, and a third from a board member, David Lamond. A few years earlier, he'd heard about us from Daniel Osorio, and called one day to tell me that he'd be at Ubuntu in a week. When I told him I wasn't planning to be in Port Elizabeth that week, he told me to make it happen, and if he liked what we were doing, it'd be worth my time. On his last day in Port Elizabeth, he told me he wanted to make a long-term commitment to Ubuntu and join our board. David always encouraged me to follow my own path and not to try to chase the trends of the development world. "I invest in you because you're you," he'd tell me, and that line stuck in my head. The Ubuntu Centre was another risk that he understood. Most significantly, Daniel Osorio, Merafe Moloto, another of our board members, and I traveled to Detroit in the middle of the winter to pitch the Kresge Foundation, which had never invested in a capital project overseas that wasn't a university or a hospital. We went in with confidence, and we left with a $650,000 grant.

~~~~~~~

Of course, the most important step in the process was finding the right architect. We wanted someone from South Africa, and we interviewed more than a dozen. When people came in for the interview, they immediately said, "Show me a picture of what you want, of a building you'd like it to resemble." When I'd try to describe it, they'd respond, "Oh, you can't build that here." That, to me, was a clear sign they weren't right for the project. Finally, someone referred me to Stan Field, an architect from Port Elizabeth who'd left during apartheid and now lived in California. I told him, "The building I want hasn't been designed yet, I want this to be a building that wins awards." And he knew what I meant.

As he explains, "Architecture is about the obvious that's never been stated. It is about the recognizable that's never been seen."* Eight minutes into our conversation, I hired him.

Stan came down to our site along with his son Jess, his partner in their firm, Field Architecture. Stan, who has a sweep of gray hair and a genial smile, spent hundred of hours talking to our staff and to com-

---

* Stan and his son Jess wrote a book, *Designing Ubuntu,* reflecting on the process and philosophy of designing the Ubuntu Centre.

munity members, finding out what they needed and wanted from this building. He had a little stool that he'd sit on out in the red dirt field, watching people walk by, interviewing anyone who would talk to him, and sketching out ideas.

At one of our first meetings to discuss architectural plans, Stan didn't bring blueprints or technical specs. He sat down at the table and sketched out a bird. He wanted the building to have wings, he said. Then he presented us with sketches of a group of concrete buildings leaning toward each other, rising organically from the landscape. The angle of the walls did have the kinetic lift of a bird's wings.

The slant of the walls gave the Ubuntu Centre a sense of vitality, of movement, but also a sense of support, of community, of *ubuntu*. "Each one of these structures is like an independent building that belongs to a family of buildings which rely on one another for support," Stan noted. "As the light changes throughout the day, the shape seems to move. Light enters between the structures, drawing people into the deep, luminous spaces. This is a living building, which people know and use daily." Unlike most structures in the townships, there's no wall with razor wire or glass shards on top to provide security; the Ubuntu Centre would be open to the street, available to all.

The grouping allowed the building to incorporate, rather than block, the pathways that locals used across the land in their day-to-day lives. As Stan observed, in an area of the city that had been left with virtually no infrastructure during apartheid, these informal byways are the heart of the community, connecting people and places. Stan would say of the Ubuntu Centre, "This is a building people went through, not to." The idea suited us perfectly: Ubuntu wasn't the destination, it was a place people could come to get to where they were going.

The material—concrete and large windows overlaid with gum-tree poles to provide shade, a traditional mode of building in the area—gave the structure sturdiness, permanence, and timelessness: It looked like a part of the community that belonged there, but also like something from the future. It relied on sustainable building techniques and solar power, so that we could operate with minimal impact on the environment. And we invested in the best technology possible in our pediatric clinic, in the wiring throughout the building, and one of the first iMac labs in the country.

Once we started to have contractors come in to work, I noticed that each one seemed a bit overwhelmed by the technical challenges of this building. We found we had to train people in new techniques of construction. The interconnectedness of all the spaces challenged them as well: You couldn't build this as a series of boxes that simply led into one another.

Jana and I together ran the project, and the rebuilding of friendship and trust between us was a welcome by-product of these months. Jana had grown into a more prominent role in the organization, and the feeling of being overlooked had begun to fade. And I'd realized all the challenges she'd faced, and that I'd failed to support her in, during her early years with Ubuntu. With the excitement of the Centre coming into being, we'd been able to put those issues away, at last.

As the Ubuntu Centre started to take shape, people passing by would stop and look at the construction, and at the rendering we had posted on a billboard outside. Even though it was materializing in front of them, it somehow seemed even stranger that this building belonged here, and not in town. I went outside once to talk to some of the children standing at the billboard. They asked me, "Why aren't you building this in town? It's a museum." That thought—that feeling of inferiority, one of the vestiges of apartheid—was exactly why we had to build this building. Slowly, as the structure rose, our dream was becoming their dream.

~~~~~~~

On a warm, sunny September day in 2010, Hugh Masekela's trumpet rang out against the clatter of township traffic. More than a thousand people swayed and clapped, calling out encouragement as a group of stomping, gyrating dancers led the way into an angular concrete building rising among the tin-roofed shacks of Zwide township, on the outskirts of Port Elizabeth, South Africa. This was the Ubuntu Centre: the new home of Ubuntu Education Fund, the culmination of years spent cajoling donors, consulting architects, wrangling unions and contractors, the manifestation of the belief that even the poorest deserve the magnificent.

The building itself exceeded all my expectations. An open doorway laid with textured tiles reflecting the colors of the dirt roads in the township led into a spacious entry area. To the left, you found the clinic, with a comfortable waiting area and private rooms for consultation. To the right, huge mahogany doors, hand carved with a spoon chisel to create a deeply textured surface that rippled with light, led to a vast community theater and hall. An enormous wall of gum poles provided an acoustic dampening effect so that music and dance performances could be heard at their best. The high ceilings and a wall of windows created a sense of infinite space and possibility. On the roof, a communal garden boasted plots of lettuces, broccoli, carrots, and cabbage.

It was a surreal moment for all of us. To look at where we had started, in a broom closet at Emfundweni Primary School, and then to see this building created a sense of vertigo. Most important, Stan had taken his conversations with each one of us and managed to create a building where every person could say, "That was my idea." We all felt ownership. One of our staff told Stan, "This building, it is going to communicate. That is the building's nature. It's there to contribute the positive, which means this building is also campaigning for us. You see? Everyone knows us because of this building. It's a magnet, you see."

And it received recognition for others, as well: As a work in progress, *Architect* magazine awarded the Ubuntu Centre its Progressive Architecture Award at a ceremony held at the Museum of Modern Art in Manhattan. One of the jury members noted, "The complex of forms is sophisticated and articulate while nonetheless being friendly."

Best of all was the reaction from our students. A young woman named Bulali, who was helping to care for seven family members, including a mother suffering from bipolar disorder, and still making it to the top of her academic class, wrote a poem to express what the building meant to her.

As Junior Jazz Tavern sat them down for a brown sparkling drink

Their hearts united

They did not notice each other's skin colour

Those two men wanted to listen to people's cries and laughter

The first smile came from a sheep's head in the fridge

And again, their New idea to Brighton the future arose

And built a home for the township

———

A mother to (orphans) (all)

———

Believe me when I Say

The walls talk

The building speaks

The deaf could hear and the blind could see

Mother Zwide giving birth to the centre of dreams

The centre of opportunities

The pride of the township

As Zwide's soil is enriched with the wise material

A building that discovers the hidden identity of you

Though they travel the road of silence

They carry no heart to hate

They offer love to strangers

Even though I look with my nose and smell with my eyes

They love me anyway

Even though diseases come to visit them

They eventually went home

'Cause they look beyond your injured heart

Yet still make it possible for your heart to smile

Though friends greet you good-bye

Continue without fear—for you know, UBUNTU is FAMILY

Then there are those who pretend to be nothing

'Cause they think they are nothing

Whilst cowardly hiding amongst all

Ubuntu sees them as everything

And the Ubuntu family has made life everything.

As your worthlessness travels another road

Your dark mind is enlightened

They prevent the lack of education

For they see that the eyes of an educated child speak success

———

Hear the walls say

I AM BECAUSE YOU ARE

Listen to the building speak

I am because of the Ubuntu that walks within me

Healing the deep wounds entailed within you

Helping a crippled heart that wishes to find peace.

Constructing small voices to mature

Making the unheard voices heard

For black and white voices to unify into one voice

For the children of South Africa and the world's to come

To be fulfilled

As each heard dreams of finding stability.

The Ubuntu Centre is a commitment to the townships and a physical embodiment of our belief that access to health care and education isn't a privilege but a right. It's a refuge for the children of the township, a place where they know they can find respite from the chaos of their lives. And yet, I know our work isn't done. Every student we interact with has a heart-wrenching story, and day in and day out we deal with traumatic situations and children who exist in a near-constant state of crisis. And for every student who finds success, there are five others who haven't, and ten others who don't even make it through our doors. Those failures—even when nothing different could be done—weigh heavily.

~~~~~~~

Sadly, Lungi had begun to look like one of those failures. As we'd feared, coming back to Port Elizabeth was difficult, and she'd cried angrily when she heard that she wouldn't be going back to DSG. We found another school in Port Elizabeth, a good private school, but she started to skip classes, would stay out with her friends and not come home until late in the evening, and she failed again.

Fezeka kept visiting her, kept urging her to find some direction in her life. We enrolled her in our Pathways Programme for students who might not be able to or want to pursue higher education, but who need help finding job training and career opportunities. But even then, Lungi refused to commit. She started to skip sessions, and would be away from home when counselors would come to follow up. Eventually, we had to suspend her from the program.

"At that moment, I was like, *Oh, they are so unfair, why are they doing this to me?*" Lungi remembers. "But when I sat down and thoroughly thought about it, actually, whatever you do, there's always a reward, there's always an answer in everything you do. In a way, this is parenthood. People can't congratulate you when you are wrong. They show you the wrong way, and show you the right way: This is wrong, this is how it's done, and when you don't listen, they punish you. That's how things work in life. It's not always easy in life, it's not always get, get, get."

Zethu, on the other hand, had continued to chart a steady course. She was aiming to be a chartered accountant, and applied to Rhodes University. But her grades didn't quite match her aspirations, and she didn't get in. She was crushed; it felt like all her hard work had been for nothing. But one of our education counselors at Ubuntu urged her to consider Nelson Mandela Metropolitan University in Port Elizabeth. He pressed the university to admit Zethu—as Zethu recalls, he told them, "If she doesn't make it in the first year, kick her out!"—and in 2009 she started her first year in managed accounting there.

But every setback for her sister felt like a personal failure. She'd question whether she was doing any good for her siblings by caring for them, when things still went wrong. And meanwhile, she needed to stay on track with her own studies. She'd invested so much in her schooling, and so many people at Ubuntu had advocated for her, she felt an equal responsibility to succeed there.

It was especially difficult for her to see what was happening with her brother. His anger and psychological problems, his inability to stay in school—as Zethu recalls, "I felt it was my fault, because I was like, *Okay, I tried my best to use the support Ubuntu is providing, but for him it is not working. Maybe I'm not there enough for him, I'm not putting much effort in helping out."*

It had become clear, though, that Star's troubles were more profound than either Zethu or Ubuntu first realized. He'd been doing very well in the school at the home where Fezeka had found him a place, so when he was discharged at eighteen, Fezeka recalls, he asked to reenroll at a neighborhood school. Fezeka convinced the principal of a township school to allow Star to start in grade eight, and he managed to complete a full year. But by the end of it, many of the same issues had cropped up again: anger, leaving home for days at a time, an inability to focus on any tasks.

Finally, he was admitted to the local hospital, and from there to an institute for mental health. As Fezeka recollects, he was diagnosed with schizophrenia and given medicine for treatment. Once the medical routine had been established, he was sent home. Fezeka made sure that the nurses at Ubuntu were able to give Star his medication, which had to be injected, and he was able to lead a fairly normal life. But at some point, he decided that the regimen was too much for him, and he stopped coming in for the medication. He was over eighteen at this point, so there was little that Ubuntu could do other than try to keep an eye on him.

Soon, he was back to wandering; he'd leave the house for days. Sometimes it seemed intentional, sometimes it seemed like he just got lost. But every time he disappeared, Zethu, Lungi, and Fezeka would wonder if he would make it home this time.

CHANGING THE CONVERSATION:
"RISK" ISN'T A FOUR-LETTER WORD

IN THE DEVELOPMENT world, organizations tend to live and die by a twelve-month grant cycle. That means that taking risks—innovating in fund-raising or programming—is by necessity discouraged. Sure, that risk might pay off big-time. But if it doesn't, or if it isn't quite a success this year but shows promise for next year, or in five years, it could mean the loss of millions of dollars in funding.

Several years ago, one of Ubuntu's donors funded a two-year education initiative. We learned a great deal from the process, but it didn't yield the results we wanted—we had known that this was a probability from the beginning, as it was a pilot. But I was extremely proud to take the two-year report to the donor and show them how much we got out of the process. We'd built a body of research that provided evidence of the need for an early-childhood program, and we were about to set out a major new programmatic initiative based on the report.

Their response? "Jake, we love Ubuntu, we want to give you major support, but we don't want to continue down this road. Give us something with quick, easy results we can show our board."

I was so disheartened. What used to drive the great charitable foundations was a culture of philanthropy that said, "We're going to invest in things no one else would invest in, to try to change society." With the current emphasis on meeting metrics, that kind of innovative, long-term thinking has diminished. Philanthropy should be driving social change, but instead, it too often only wants guaranteed returns.

But let's look at what putting in years of struggle, years of mistakes and debate, and taking risks has earned us. In 2011, McKinsey and Company analyzed Ubuntu's practices and looked closely at the economic impact our programs had for individuals and the community. They found that a $1.00 investment in Ubuntu produces a net gain for society of $2.20. That dollar, for an individual child, means real lifetime earnings of $8.70. These aren't results you'll see in a year's time, but they make a lasting difference in a community.

— —

Stan Field is a California-based architect who, with his son Jess, designed the award-winning Ubuntu Centre. Born in Port Elizabeth, South Africa, he received his master's in architecture from the University of Pennsylvania. He was appointed the chief architect for the city of Jerusalem in 1978, then relocated to Palo Alto, California, in 1990. Stan is best known for integrating environmental and cultural contexts into his work. In 2012, he was chosen as the Sophia Gray Laureate, an honor that recognizes a South African architect's contribution to society.

Why as a society are we so afraid of risk?

FIELD: Any pursuit that is worthwhile involves risk. Our fear, though, is around failure. I remember when my son Jess was defending his dissertation in front of all of these professors from Harvard and other Ivy League schools. During his presentation, one of the professors said, "Wow, what you are doing is really like surfing and being one with the wave." I remember that Jess just looked a little puzzled after he said this. After five minutes, Jess came back to that question and said he wanted to correct the professor about what the surfer is actually doing. He said that when you are surfing, you are anticipating these waves that are coming all the way from Hawaii to the Pacific Coast [of California, where we live]. When the wave hits and you begin to ride it, you are constantly on the edge of failure and so close to falling. But, as Jess said, instead of giving up, this is what propels him forward. And it is at this tiny precipice between success and failure that the great, innovative ideas are born.

Failure doesn't always have to be negative—there is a positive side to it as well. Too often we set in stone what success will look like for an endeavor, but what we need to remember is that following a strong process allows for adaptation and change, which can make an end product look a lot different than the original vision.

Too often we focus on the challenges as opposed to the solutions. We don't allow people to dream. How do you see your own work counteracting this tendency?

FIELD: Architecture has the power to be transformative and to shift the way that people think about their own reality and the world beyond them. I like to think of it as time being recorded by what has been built. As an architect, I want to be innovative and want to define history by the buildings that I am helping to create. Periods of history are defined by what is built, but they are also defined by the great social innovations that emerge. We need to create an

(continued)

environment that allows people to think outside the box and not be afraid to address our biggest problems.

Did you see the Ubuntu Centre as a risk?

FIELD: No, I saw it as an adventure. I never saw the Ubuntu Centre as a risk, and neither did you—and I think that's part of why I wanted to work with you. It was challenging, exciting, exhilarating. Zwide township had never seen a building like this. In fact, I think you would be pretty hard-pressed to find a building of this quality of design in any disadvantaged community in the world. How sad is that?

For us, it was not about the final product, but about the process. I remember talking to you, Banks, the entire Ubuntu family, and the people of Zwide about what they envisioned for the Ubuntu Centre—what their hopes and dreams were. The voices that we heard began slowly to impart the real needs facing the community. We encountered so many hardships and had so many failed attempts, but without acknowledging our mistakes, we would not have been as successful as we were. When embarking on a project as massive as the Ubuntu Centre, you have to be open-minded in your vision—you can't follow every rule, stick to every plan, or listen to only your own idea.

I think that, by nature, people view innovation as riskier. And that's what the Ubuntu Centre was—an innovation—and that's why people were so reticent to accept it. To us, it seemed groundbreaking, but to others, it seemed unattainable. You and Banks also adopted a bottom-up approach and ensured that your clients were just as involved in the process as you were. Most companies embrace a top-down approach. I think that the fact that you were doing things differently made your endeavor seem riskier. Also, I believe that setting goals is one way to minimize risk, but achieving much more than the stated goals is a huge risk. And that's exactly what we were trying to do when building the Ubuntu Centre—exceed our own and the community's expectations.

Stan, you never really use the word "risk," but instead talk about "adventure." From a personal standpoint, how have you applied this spirit of adventure to your life and the decisions you've made?

FIELD: Well, I think that South Africa breeds a spirit of adventure. Having grown up there, I was fascinated by its history—the wars, the mix of cultures, the sense of humanity that existed. However, as I got older, I started to feel as though I didn't have a voice—the white government didn't want to listen to people like me and the blacks didn't want any sort of white patronage. To try and find my place as part of the country, I entered a competition to design a low-income housing project in the Cape Flats of Cape Town. After I lost, I decided to go discover my roots in Israel and truly went from the frying pan into the fire.

Following that, I embarked on another adventure and journeyed to the United States, where I further developed my architecture career. When you approached me with the Ubuntu Centre idea, I knew I had to go back to South Africa. You see, Africa's in my blood, Israel is in my heart, and, well, I haven't quite figured out where America is. But I do feel at home in all three places. It's a wonderful feeling to have so many different environments, ecologies, and cultures form a core part of who I am. Each of these experiences was formative in its own way and none was like the other—without any one of them, I think I would be a very different person.

From a personal perspective, what do you think sets you apart from other individuals? You seem to have an ability to walk into these contentious environments with such confidence. Many people would perceive your experiences as risky, but you don't.

FIELD: I can say that the common thread throughout my life been a sense of shared humanity—I think that is why Ubuntu resonated so much with me. It's hard to impart or to communicate, but this sense of human interconnectedness does exist everywhere you go. I like to call it the "rolling smile"—when someone thinks you are smiling at them and they smile back at somebody [else]. It's infectious and it's a beautiful thing. I think that this ability to connect with people—no matter where they are from—is what has made the transition to different environments and cultures so easy for me.

CHAPTER TEN

The
Pathway

ONE WINTER WEEKEND IN 2012, I TRAVELED TO UPSTATE NEW YORK AS A
new member of the Clinton Global Initiative (CGI) advisory board, a
group of forty nonprofit and business leaders, academics, and policy
wonks. We were gathering to talk about how to make a "real" difference
in the developing world. On the first morning of the retreat, President
Clinton made a speech detailing the successes of the CGI and calling for
further commitment from all of us. Following his speech, over breakfast, Clinton asked me what I thought of his vision for the CGI's future.

As most would when answering a former president of the United
States, an incredibly charismatic leader and perhaps the most promi-
nent philanthropic activist of our time, I came up with an endorsement:
"Sir, it was incredibly motivating."

Clinton gave me a skeptical look and said, "I didn't bring you here
to tell me I gave a good speech. Tell me what you thought."

For better or worse, it doesn't take much to entice me to be candid.

I told him, "I actually think it's irresponsible to say that CGI 'positively impacts' four hundred million people."

Clinton peered at me over his glasses and asked, "What do you mean?"

"It probably would be more accurate to say that it positively affects forty million people, if you are measuring it by true, sustainable impact in their lives—and that's just as impressive as making a small difference in a larger number of lives. I mean, if you give four hundred million people a cracker, it might positively impact their hunger at that moment, but it doesn't change anything about their situation."

President Clinton laughed and nodded. He understood what I was getting at and quickly began asking me pointed questions about how, then, Ubuntu could widen its influence. As ever, I marveled at the agility of his mind and felt awed by his mastery of the subtlest nuances in development. President Clinton's influence on development in the past decade-plus cannot be overstated. He's the model of an activist statesman. I feel incredibly proud to be in a position to share my vision of development with someone like President Clinton.

I see every day the difference we are making in kids' lives, kids who don't get a fraction of the opportunities my children will likely take for granted. A couple of years ago, I sat in Ubuntu's offices in Zwide township with seven girls who had just graduated from university—seven of our first students. That's what it's about: seven kids in thirteen years. The nonprofit sector is driven by growth, growth, growth—defined narrowly as geographical expansion and numbers served—at the expense, way too often, of quality. But we're okay with the fact that we're not, and will never be, everywhere. We're still trying to change the world; but we're doing it by focusing on one corner of it. We don't claim ours is the only way, but it's the best way we've found to help children who are at the bottom of the bottom begin to compete with those who have every advantage imaginable.

In 2014, we celebrated our fifteenth anniversary. For a long time, I would ask myself, *Was it worth it?* I spent weeks at a time away from my family; at one point, my wife's colleagues didn't believe she actually had a husband, because for two years, I missed every one of her work functions. We have two sons now, and I know there are times when Lindsay resents how often I'm gone. When you get married and have kids, you expect you and your spouse to be partners, but here I am raising other people's kids. One day, my older son saw a plane go overhead while we were out on the playground, and he said, "Papa, you live up there, right?" So I've changed: These days, I'm in South Africa every six weeks, and I'll fly out on a Sunday and back on Friday so I'm home for the weekend.

And, in the end, this is my passion. As hard as it's been to conjure this organization from nothing, I can't imagine doing anything else. Ultimately, our model works. If you invest in a child, no matter how broken or abused, the way you would in your own, and treat him with the same dignity and respect, that child has an infinitely greater chance to make it.

Around our tenth anniversary, as our older students began looking at university, it became apparent that, even with our intervention, a significant achievement gap existed for the township high school students. Our best students showed great progress, but it wasn't enough. We tried intensive after-school tutoring, but despite this added support, most grade-ten students would test at a grade-seven or -eight level in math and literacy. As disheartening as this news was, we had approached the problem systematically, and the results showed us a way forward. We needed to start earlier.

One day, Jana gathered her team in a conference room and told them that they all knew what the problem was, and what they needed to do: Start an early-childhood program. Bongi Mabusela, now our early-childhood education manager, recalls, "Oh! The excitement in the team. It was like, 'This will be the best thing that will happen in this organization.'"

Ramping up the program took time, and it wasn't easy to find support networks, or even teachers, in South Africa. As has so often happened with Ubuntu, we looked around and realized that what we needed was right under our noses. We knew we had to incorporate our psychosocial, clinical, and household supports into the new program. "We would want a [teacher] who is open to the idea that a child needs to be taken care of in a holistic way and really be willing to get their hands dirty in caring about that psychosocial aspect and the health aspect of their lives as well," Bongi recalls. "I remember the conversation we had with Jana. She said, 'We have been looking around, but we actually have the right people right here.' The counselors were already involved in the after-school program, and it works having both a person who knows about their psychosocial needs and their educational needs. She said, 'We're going to take the counselors we have and we're going to provide the training they need to become teachers.'"

And we looked outside of the local context to find models, seeking support from organizations like the Barnard College Center for Toddler Development and the charter-school group KIPP. Christine Downton, a board member of Atlantic Philanthropies, gave us a small discretionary grant to spend six months visiting more than sixty early-childhood development programs across Britain, the United States, and South Africa. We visited the poorest programs and those with every resource imaginable, looking for best practices and what would fit into the context of our community. Based on all this research, we decided to introduce a play-based curriculum, which allows students to direct their day based on their own areas of interest, and maintained a high level of parental involvement, including conferences, classes on parenting skills, and time spent in the classroom. The ambition to create a program of this quality was unprecedented on the continent of Africa.

~~~~~~

Like the pathways that formed the heart of the Ubuntu Centre, helping create pathways through life has been essential to our work at

Ubuntu. Now, when a child enters the Ubuntu Centre for the first time, she becomes a part of our pathway, an innovative system that tracks each client and customizes a program of care for her and her family. Every detail of a family's care is thought of: the safety of the home, the health of everyone living there, vision and dental care, emotional and psychosocial support that also assesses the risk of abuse. We give school-age children uniforms, make sure that the adults can get to jobs or appointments, and advocate for government grants and access to social services for the families.

In essence, we provide time: hours and hours of clinic visits, of tutoring, of support groups, of counseling, and above all, of conversation. The kind of conversation a parent and child might have around the dinner table: How's school going? Who are your friends? What are you excited about? What's making you unhappy?

It's not the typical model for an NGO: So much of the development world is focused on providing tangible items, like classrooms or computers, in part because they're much easier to raise funds for. Telling someone that they are funding one hundred computers to go into township schools feels more solid than telling them that they are funding one hundred hours of time spent with a child. But a parent would never think of satisfying his own child's needs with "Oh, I'll just give him a math book or a computer program, and he'll be fine." The intensive nature of our programs doesn't come cheap: For example, we spend up to $11,000 per year per child for the three- to four-year-olds in our early-childhood program. That's because we provide intensive health, education, psychosocial, and stability services every day of the year, not only during the school year—just like a parent would.

~~~~~~~

We realized that, as essential as creating a pathway for each client, we also needed to create a pathway for our staff members. Everyone wants to know his future. What am I doing now that will get me to where I want to be in five years, and what else should I be doing along the way?

We'd made progress toward defining the roles of the senior leadership, and what we set out to do now was to make sure roles throughout the organization were well defined, that training and further education were available to all, and that each staff member felt that he was building experience and expertise so he could grow as an employee. This movement to professionalize went through its own growing pains. We'd often—and still do—talk about Ubuntu as a family, because we share a close bond based on the intensity of the work we do. But you can't fire aunts or uncles, brothers or sisters because they aren't fulfilling their role adequately. "Team" seemed like the better word: We all had to understand that our individual goals needed to serve a common purpose, and hard decisions some-times had to be made in order to obtain it. Making this distinction isn't easy, though, because we all work hard and rely on one another in a way that feels as though it transcends business.

Yet, despite some hurt feelings and anxiety over our new direction, in 2010 the staff welcomed a new initiative to provide more robust staff development, excellent medical care for everyone in the organization, and a new performance management system to create individualized plans for each staff member.

We called it BUILD—the Bertha-Ubuntu Internal Leadership Development—because we created it in partnership with the Bertha Foundation; the South African family who had established the founda-tion had been a cornerstone supporter since our first days as an organi-zation. BUILD was one of the foundation's first big initiatives, and we worked closely with Lara Tabatznik on it. She had been a key employee in our New York office for three years, running all of our events, when she left to run her family's foundation. Another former Ubuntu employee who had run our New York office, Laura Horowitz, joined her and was instrumental in launching BUILD. On our side, Craig Panell worked intensively on the project in Ubuntu's South Africa office. Initially hired as a consultant, he threw himself into the project, jettisoned his other clients, and became an integral part of our team. Together, we invested $500,000 to combine the spirit of *ubuntu* that had always guided us with world-class human-resource services.

We'd always aimed to hire from the local community, and we continue to do so; 95 percent of our staff come from the townships in which we worked. At the beginning, many of them were hired without the qualifications that, on paper, would make them good employees. We hired people with passion, with energy, and with a sense of pride in their work. Now, as attaining higher education becomes more possible for men and women from the townships, we recruit local staff members who have bachelor's degrees, who are social workers, clinicians, psychologists.

Fezeka might not have been hired elsewhere, based on her résumé. Before she joined Ubuntu, she was working in a hair salon, and had only a high school education. We gave her the training she needed to work first as a health educator, then as a counselor for high-need clients like Zethu and her siblings. Fezeka's natural intelligence and empathy shone through in each interaction, out in the field and in the office. The structure of BUILD made her path from counselor to senior manager more apparent: It was clear what she needed to do in each role, and what she wanted to accomplish and what Ubuntu needed, in turn, from her. Now she's working on a bachelor's degree in health science and social services, and serves as a senior manager in monitoring and evaluation.

~~~~~~

In 2013, another member on the BUILD pathway was Zethu. After passing all her exams and graduating with her diploma in managed accounting, she came to work at Ubuntu in the external relations department. She helped prepare for donor visits and do research to find new donors. Her ready smile and bright spirit were a welcome addition to our department.

One day in August 2013, Zethu walked from her desk to the Ubuntu Centre clinic to greet President Clinton, who, along with Chelsea Clinton and other delegates from the Clinton Foundation, was spending the day touring the Ubuntu Centre, visiting our early-education classrooms, and hearing more about our programs. Immediately, he wanted to see Zethu. They met outside the clinic. He took Zethu's hand and, hearing that she'd recently graduated from university, told her, "I am so proud of you."

Zethu was no longer the tiny schoolgirl who, in her carefully pressed school uniform, had moved a room full of powerful people with her poise and spirit. She was a young woman, professional and accomplished, who had worked diligently to find a path for herself while providing for her siblings.

Zethu accompanied President Clinton on a private plane to Pretoria for a conference, where she sat on a panel and talked about her experiences as a child head of household. The name of the panel was well suited for her: Embrace Tomorrow. She hadn't expected to be in the spotlight that day, and she froze on stage, but afterward, President Clinton told her, "Zethu, you were very good."

"He really believes in me," Zethu said, pleased and amazed. "It's people like that that keep you going."

The next year, Zethu left us for a new job at a training, human resources, and consulting group. It was the right step for her, but we were sad to see her leave. She's been an integral part of Ubuntu for many years. It seems clear, though, that Zethu will never entirely leave Ubuntu, in the same way that no child ever fully leaves her family. "Ubuntu is just a heartwarming job, knowing you have made a difference in someone's life," Zethu told me recently. "On my Facebook, kids are crying, 'We don't see you anymore at Ubuntu, what has happened to you?' I still speak to them on Facebook if they have problems. Even though I'm not on the counseling team, these kids see me as someone that they can relate to."

Lungi had found a new pathway as well. She'd auditioned for, and gotten, a job as a presenter at a radio station, giving advice to other teenagers. On her first radio show, Lungi was overcome with nerves and unable to talk; her producer had had to take over. But with a little practice, she felt more natural on the air, and her quick wit and charisma worked well on the radio program. Then the producer of the show told her she needed to get back to school: After all, she gave advice to other teenagers, and she needed to be a role model for them.

She enrolled in a government school in Motherwell, a nearby township, to repeat grade ten. Ubuntu worked with Lungi to create a budget and allocate her money carefully, and she was able to pay for her own uniform and school fees. She and Zethu live together in the modest Reconstruction and Development Programme home that their mother had applied for before her death and that they were able to move into several years ago.

"Our saying, that your birthplace shouldn't determine your future, I like that," Zethu said. "It speaks to me as a person. Because I'm staying now in my mother's house, but the place we were before, where we had to share with another family, it wasn't nice.

"I've managed to put tiling in my home, I've managed to put a stove in my home, I've managed to buy a TV for my home, and I'm proud of that." She added, "What is special about Ubuntu is that you are on the pathway until you have succeeded. Now I'm a successful graduate, earning my own income, having my own budget, having my own salary."

As a sister and a mother, Zethu can't imagine living apart from Lungi. "Sometimes, I know that there will be that day when I would leave and live my own life, and she will live her own life as well. But sometimes I feel scared—will she be able to live without me? Because it is very difficult for me to let her go, and it is very difficult as well to let her do her own decisions."

For her part, Lungi can see now what hard work and sacrifice Zethu poured into caring for her and Star. "I didn't know the difference between a mother and a sister, because my parents died at a very early age," Lungi told me recently. "But half of her life was about us, which is something incredible."

For Star, things continued to be difficult. Fezeka and Zethu watched unhappily as, unwilling to stay on his medication, he would wander away from home for days at a time. Sometimes, Lungi would see him at a distance in the townships, but when she would call out to him, he'd run away. After many months of not seeing Star, the sisters feared the worst; eventually, they discovered that he'd been arrested for burglary and faced prison time. They were devastated, though relieved to know that he was alive. Throughout his trial, and while he served out his sentence, Zethu visited him regularly—the first time in years that she knew exactly where he would be.

Zethu and her family represent so much about Ubuntu: the vulnerability, the potential, and the determination of the children we work with every day. But they also represent the challenges we face and the many factors that are totally out of our control. We can't promise success with every child. Like any parent, we offer unconditional support, care, and understanding. If a child fails, we'll do everything we can to help her rebound, but we also set boundaries and limits with all of our students. And sometimes, as much as it hurts, there's nothing we can do. But we still keep trying.

<p style="text-align:center">~~~~~~</p>

Ubuntu Education Fund got its start in the summer of 1998, in the red pleather seats of a *shebeen*. Apartheid was over, but the effects were still palpable in the townships: poverty, overcrowding, unemployment, and insufficient social services.

That fateful evening in the *shebeen,* I met Banks—a black South African twenty years my senior who invited me into his home based only on shared passions for soccer and education. Banks had lived his entire life in the townships, and, of course, he'd never shared a roof with a white person. He had a family, and limited means. But without hesitation, he extended an invitation to share his flat for the next four months.

What followed were some of the most incredible, eye-opening, idyllic, risky, insane months of my life. I probably should have been more cautious, but I wasn't; the people of the township might have been suspicious of me, but they weren't. I'd heard of *ubuntu*, but it was the first time I'd really seen it in action, and felt its effect on my own life.

When I got back to university, everyone assumed that as the experience in the townships faded so would my determination to work there. It didn't. Banks and I kept talking, and planning, and soon I found myself, newly graduated, canvassing the townships to find out what, exactly, we should do with Ubuntu Education Fund. We set up our offices in a broom closet, and paid our few employees in cash. We opened up one computer center, then another; started a health initiative; planned libraries; ran summer camps. We had long, tedious meetings with school officials and parents that didn't seem to accomplish much, but earned us the confidence of the community, who saw how seriously we took their input. We grew; we moved offices; we hired new people; we left the schools, but stayed true to our mission.

Over the years, I've had the good fortune of getting to meet some of my personal heroes, like Archbishop Desmond Tutu. He's been our patron now for nine years, but I still get a thrill out of seeing him. A few years ago, I spent the evening at 10 Downing Street in London, where the archbishop was speaking at an event hosted by then–prime minister Gordon Brown and his wife, Sarah. When Archbishop Tutu came into the room, the first thing he said was "Jacob, what are you doing here?"

I was, like, "Arch, you invited me!" I don't lack for confidence, but even I never imagined that Archbishop Tutu would ever know my name.

And now: We have a beautiful, symbolic home in the Ubuntu Centre. We run our own clinic. We provide meals and fresh food from our gardens, and nutritional counseling. We work with pregnant women and babies, teenagers and university students, grannies and aunties and uncles. We're grassroots, but we're fully professionalized. We have the capability to generate monthly reports that help us allocate our resources in a way that's flexible and responsive to outcomes, that relies on facts and not just our gut. We're not afraid to take a risk on a new approach, see how it works, and then cut it if it doesn't.

If I had to distill the lessons we've learned into a few major points, it would look something like this.

Listen. This gets invoked a lot, but it's rare to find it in practice. Listen to the people you are serving. Listen to your staff. Listen to your leadership team. Hear what experiences and needs all these people who make up the fabric of your organization have, and then craft a thoughtful response to them. Yes, you might hear a lot that isn't helpful, but the best ideas float to the top when given the opportunity. And through listening and reacting, that push and pull, you create a living organization that can adapt to the world around it. The worst thing to happen to any organization is to get stuck in its ways, or to do something just because it's the way it has always been done. By listening to the people around you, the ones most intimately involved in the work you are doing, you can respond to new circumstances or find better ways to address old ones.

Fail. Some of the most important progress we make comes directly out of our failures. Create an environment in which the most important thing is to learn and then improve, rather than hit targets, and innovation will flourish. Nonprofits tend to be risk averse, for fear of losing donors and funding if certain markers of success aren't met. Yet with confidence in your core mission and in your organization's ability to fulfill that mission, even if not every program thrives, you can get people to invest in *your* vision, not in their own.

Be optimistic. A belief that tomorrow will be better, and the day after tomorrow even better still—that kind of optimism propels a nonprofit entrepreneur forward despite long odds and vocal doubters. This work requires long hours, inadequate compensation, and constant obstacles. You have to believe that what you are doing will work, that it may take weeks or months or years of ridiculously hard work but, ultimately, you can make a difference. Part of this optimism requires a strong vision: an ability to see a future no one else can see, and a commitment to making that vision come to life.

Make a statement. Don't be afraid to make a bold declaration of your beliefs and intentions. For us, it was the Ubuntu Centre. With that building, we told our staff and our community that we were here to stay, that they deserved the best, and that an investment in them was a sound one. We told our donors that we were determined to think big, even if it seemed crazy. And we told the development community that it was possible to envision a different way of operating in the context of poverty. Yes, being bold might turn some people off. But it also draws in the people who will believe in you and support you for years, through all kinds of ups and downs.

Don't undermine yourself. Always hold yourself to a high standard, and demand that others hold you to a high standard. Especially in the early days, this is tough, and we certainly undermined ourselves (accepting those outdated encyclopedias and filled-in coloring books for our first library comes to mind). But every time you allow yourself to accept something second-rate, or to let a donor set program goals in return for their money, you undermine your mission. Define your own goals and standards, and don't waver.

Nurture strong leadership. Not one leader—leaders. A singular vision may be essential for beginning and sustaining the start-up phase of an organization, but in order to develop, you need a team of people who bring diverse strengths and distinct points of view. Giving space to others to have great ideas and execute them is essential to the longevity and the robustness of any organization. But in nonprofits, where people are driven by passion not a desire to make money, getting that sense of buy-in is crucial to attracting and retaining the best staff. I spend a lot of time with the members of my leadership team and give a lot of thought to what will motivate and inspire them. When salary isn't the be-all and end-all, knowing that they are integral to the organization not only helps retain talent but also makes sure that we are all working at our best.

Know the key players. The clearest vision for change will falter if you don't identify and learn to work with the other people who will help make it happen. You have to invest the time in building relationships in order to start something from nothing. This includes the people inside your organization (the staff members who have the drive and ability to make each initiative work); the people outside your organization who support it (board members and donors); the people who make decisions that impact your work (government and community leaders); and the people in the development world who set the agenda for the industry (thought leaders and influencers who can mentor, support, and help you navigate your way toward accomplishing your goals). Knowing how to get their attention and find ways to make them *want* to help you opens doors to both the opportunities you know you want and the ones you didn't even know existed.

It's not uncommon to hear people in the nonprofit world say, "Let's work ourselves out of a job." It seems logical—to be so success-ful that there's no need for your particular support in a community. But if you have been that effective, you've clearly created a hell of an infrastructure, and it would be a shame to lose all that that entails. Yes, we can see a future when the area we work in has evolved into a middle-class enclave where people are more concerned about what university their child will get into than where their next meal will come from. But needs, if different ones, will still exist, for tutoring and leadership training, for after-school activities, and for university scholarships. If we succeed as an organization, part of that success must be evolution, not extinction.

~~~~~~~~

These days, I look at Ubuntu and feel overwhelmed by what we've accomplished and how many people have been with us along the way. From a chance encounter in a *shebeen* to building the Ubuntu Centre, from two men transcending differences to a global network of support, it's been an amazing ride.

Of course, we've made our share of mistakes, and we still make them. I can think of many decisions I'd make differently if I could. I know I mistreated people along the way, and made choices that hurt people. I can't forget the staff members and children who didn't make it, who disappeared or died. But above all, I was always trying to do what I thought was best for the organization; we learn from our failures, and we keep improving. And now, I can stand on a stage at our gala and look around at five hundred people who have all bought in to what we are doing.

What helps keep me going, day after day, is that I'm surrounded and supported by friends and family, from my colleagues to our supporters. Seeing friends find success and then channel that success toward our mission has been touching and affirming—like my high-school friend Philip Vassiliou, who approached me in 2008 about getting more involved with Ubuntu. He'd moved to Dubai and had done well in the finance-sector there; over the years he'd been a donor, but now he wanted to do more, and in 2009 he joined our board. Everyone from my grandmother and her friends, to cousins and aunts and uncles, to my mother-in-law (of all people, one of my biggest champions) and dozens of friends from all phases of my life, have joined us as donors, volunteers, or members of our board.

More than anything, I love this feeling: that we all—staff, donors, clients—have created this landslide of compassion and generosity, this expression of *ubuntu*. This experience has allowed me to be an optimist about our world, because every day I get to see that when people come together, good things happen.

Nelson Mandela, respectfully known by his clan name, Madiba, meant a great deal to me. His struggle, along with that of other freedom fighters, piqued my interest in South Africa, his policies of inclusion and humanity galvanized me when I visited South Africa for the first time, in the wake of the first free elections, and his ability to listen to other viewpoints and respect other cultures moved me to stay. And Madiba lived a life that was intrinsically bound to the lives of his countrymen. His famous words continue to inspire: "What counts in life is not the mere fact that we have lived. It is what difference we have made to the lives of others that will determine the significance of the life we lead."

And the circle grows. Not long ago, we hosted the first meeting of the Ubuntu Alumni Network. Forty-one young men and women came together in our hall and began to figure out what their new roles will be in the organization, how they can give back. What thrilled me the most was the question one of the alumni asked Ciko Thomas and Ziyanda Ntshona, Ubuntu board members originally from the townships who attended the meeting as well. "How do you get on the board?" this young woman asked. "Because that's one of my lifetime goals."

CHANGING THE CONVERSATION:
THE BIGGER PICTURE

OVER THE YEARS at Ubuntu, we've found ourselves diverging from some of the most prevalent ideas in the nonprofit industry. Our practical experience showed us that the conventional wisdom often didn't work on the ground, and we didn't hesitate to rethink the most commonly accepted practices.

As we continue to work, it's helpful to step back from the particular and think more globally about our own and others' practices. What have we done well? What have been our failures? Why, with billions of dollars dedicated to poverty relief, has so little progress been made? What gives us hope for the future? I certainly don't have all the answers, but I think keeping this conversation going is the surest way to see our way forward.

Fred Swaniker is the founder of the African Leadership Academy, the African Leadership Network, and the African Leadership University, all of which identify and nurture the next generation of ethical and engaged African leaders. Born in Ghana, he has lived and worked throughout Africa, and earned an MBA from Stanford University. In 2010, he was among 115 young entrepreneurs selected to meet President Barack Obama at the first President's Forum with Young African Leaders, and Forbes included him as one of their top ten "youngest power men" in Africa in 2011. He's been recognized for his work by the World Economic Forum, Echoing Green, and the Aspen Institute.

What has the nonprofit sector done well over the past decade?

SWANIKER: The past ten years have given rise to the iPhone, Facebook, and wireless routers; this decade of technological innovation has been one of the most prolific in a century. Recently, nonprofits have started to leverage these advancements, integrating them into their programs. The Ushahidi team in Kenya, for instance, developed a system that uses e-mails and text messages to track instances of electoral violence. They created a "crowdmap" of the country, plotting reports across cities and villages. This not only allowed international organizations to monitor voting but also established levels of transparency and accountability that had not previously existed in the country. Innovations like

(continued)

these have yielded extraordinary results, and I hope to see a lot of growth in these ventures, particularly the many tech incubators across the continent.

Even with these innovative strategies, why do you think that the industry hasn't made nearly as much progress toward eradicating poverty as we had hoped?

SWANIKER: Too many nonprofit leaders implement patchwork solutions that trap them in a vicious cycle of responding to rather than eradicating systemic challenges. Organizations distribute food aid, but recipient communities will be hungry again in six months unless the next great African scientist discovers how to improve crop yields or African politicians create effective incentive policies to promote development of agricultural infrastructure. Yet the urgency of crises like famines galvanizes philanthropists to donate to short-term solutions that produce immediate results, while murkier, more intangible challenges that are often the root cause of such emergencies attract far less support. But if we want to solve the world's most pressing problems, we will have to find a better balance between funding disaster relief and diverting resources to developing sustainable long-term approaches.

How can we shift this mentality?

SWANIKER: In reference to African development, specifically, we have to start with listening to Africans and reducing skepticism surrounding the "African NGO." There are certainly mismanaged grassroots organizations out there (there are in every country), but there are also so many effective models that have to go through twice as much scrutiny to receive the same amount of money as their Western counterparts. Given all the misconceptions surrounding Africa, these nonprofits have almost no credibility without ties to Europe or America. I doubt that the African Leadership Academy would have been successful had I not graduated from Macalester College and Stanford University. My American education legitimizes my approach and builds trust with donors. Yet, other equally impactful organizations are pigeonholed because they do not have any connections to the West. Donors do not trust that they will spend contributions appropriately. This problem continues to derail development across Africa.

We must focus on counteracting this bias and celebrating smaller but incredibly effective nonprofits. Their work should be highlighted on the international conference circuit, and their voices should be heard. African nonprofit leaders, more than anyone else in the industry, understand their communities' needs; they have the expertise and experience to achieve this balance between long- and short-term challenges. We have to make a greater effort to empower them. A possible solution to this problem could involve establishing an intermediary Western firm that fund-raises on behalf of community-based nonprofits. The institution would do due diligence on the organizations it supports and thereby legitimize and expose African nonprofits to Western donors. Then, as more and more of these grassroots models flourish, we could do away with the intermediary institution.

What types of investments should we make?

SWANIKER: Whenever I am asked this question, I always think of a favorite quote from John D. Rockefeller, "Charity is injurious unless it helps the recipient to become independent of it." Philanthropists have to respect Africans enough to want them to eventually not rely on their money and to let go of a need to "save" people. I don't doubt that this will take an immense amount of self-confidence from donors.

Moving forward, their investments should focus on building independence; they should fund strategies that empower disadvantaged communities to thrive without the help of nonprofits ever again. For me, these approaches are all about people and investing in their brains. Once you educate a child, you give her something that can never be taken away from her. You provide her with something that will continue to benefit her for fifty to a hundred years. Quality academic programs—not just building a school or handing out textbooks—can build leaders that will have the capacity to develop long-term solutions to systemic challenges like food insecurity.

What challenges do nonprofits face in the coming decade?

SWANIKER: Financial sustainability; nonprofits spend far too much time fund-raising. When venture firms invest in start-up companies in Silicon Valley, they make long-term financial commitments and expect CEOs to spend 100 percent of their time building the company. They look for profitable results within three to five years. Yet nonprofits must constantly solicit donations; there are few philanthropists that give significant multiyear donations.

(continued)

Organizations are trapped in twelve-month grant cycles that require them to demonstrate progress every six months. They waste so much time, human capital, and stress navigating these timelines. Their CEOs devote more than 50 percent of their energy to traveling around the world, overseeing events, and making asks rather than focusing on the social challenges they founded their organizations to mitigate.

What makes you hopeful about the future?

SWANIKER: When I graduated from university, very few students went into the nonprofit sector; those that did were low performers without better options. The top 10 percent of my class started their own companies or competed for lucrative opportunities in finance, law, and business. But this generation is opting out of traditionally successful careers, prioritizing meaningful experiences over six-figure salaries. Millennials have watched their parents chase money only to feel, years later, unfulfilled. Many, then, are no longer interested in working for Goldman Sachs or Deloitte; rather, the best and the brightest are launching their own social enterprises and using their tremendous talents to create water sanitation technology rather than apps. Even more are applying to Teach for America and entry-level assistant positions at the smallest NGOs. The development industry's ability to attract and capitalize on this talent will spawn enormous growth. Brilliant minds that are more focused on reducing climate change or curing HIV/AIDS than expanding market shares or increasing quarterly returns for stakeholders give me hope for the future.

EPILOGUE

FROM THE BEGINNING, WE'VE SPENT A LOT OF TIME THINKING ABOUT what Ubuntu's responsibility to the wider world of development might be. People have urged us to "go to scale" from the day we started.

In our early years, especially, these proposals tempted us: It felt like acceptance into the cool clique at school. For a nonprofit, the way to feel like you've made it in a crowded field is to raise more money and reach more and more people—that's how you get noticed. In 2002 and 2003, as our work in the schools clearly made a difference in the education and health of the children who attended them, government officials approached us about expanding Ubuntu throughout the Eastern Cape, South Africa's second largest province and home to more than six million people. They gave us the full-court press: chauffeured us to meetings in fancy government-owned cars, took us out to lunches, and offered us 10 million rand (at the time, about $1.5 million). We devoted about a year to exploring the possibility of running Ubuntu programs throughout the province.

As we looked into it, though, we kept running up against the problem of our own capacity to ramp up that dramatically. We simply didn't have the infrastructure in place to do it effectively. We kept trying to talk ourselves around that roadblock. But then I traveled to Alice, a town some 150 miles northeast of Port Elizabeth. I met with some of the people from the local schools and other community members. It was a pleasant meeting, but I thought, "I don't know *any* of these people." And they looked at me as though they were thinking, "Who the hell are you?" Part of what makes Ubuntu successful is our deep connection to the community we work in. So we passed on this tempting offer.

Over the years, we had other offers to "franchise" Ubuntu—to let

other people use our name and our model to open up their own branch
in another community. Again, it was tempting. But even if it were someone else running the day-to-day, we'd have to be involved. It's our name,
and our idea, and that would mean resources on our end. We knew that
getting bigger wouldn't help us do what we do best, and would dilute
our model. More important, franchising, in my mind, promotes medi-
ocrity. I don't want to invest in the manager who is opening up the ten
thousandth Subway. I'm sure that person does a good job, but there's no
innovation: You just serve up the same sandwich. I want to invest in the
next David Chang.

When we look at our strengths and weaknesses, what we see is
that we are quite good at delivering health care, providing education,
and offering social services, but we aren't the best organization in any
of those areas. However, what we've managed to do better than most
others is to build a community institution. We have taken a grassroots
model and systemized it in a way that no one has ever done before.

And, particularly in the past five years, I've found myself in a position to mentor others, to meet regularly with young people starting
their own organizations. I've never been asked about a situation that
I haven't experienced, and to be able to share those experiences has
been transformative, for me and for them. Now that we have a fifteen-
year-long body of work to draw from, we feel a pressing need to begin
to share it.

All this has led us to what we think will be the next big step for
Ubuntu: the Ubuntu Institute. We want to find remarkable community
builders from across the globe that we can enroll in a two-year incubator in order to provide them with knowledge, advice, mentoring, and
development. These sorts of incubators exist for small businesses, and
even for social entrepreneurs, but there are no incubators out there
for grassroots development leaders. This isn't a spin-off of Ubuntu,
or an entirely separate organization. This is an extension of what we
already do: We'll just be applying the philosophy we use in working

with children—that there is no one-size-fits-all solution, and that going deeper with a smaller number produces better long-term results—to working with other community-based organizations. And the Ubuntu Institute would put those leadership teams at the center of their own development, exactly as we've done in the townships.

We're not looking to create mini-Ubuntus, or to brand other organizations in our image. We want to reduce the loneliness that is felt in the community-development world, where it can sometimes feel like everybody has to reinvent the wheel every day, and to increase the free exchange of ideas and support among peers and colleagues. We'd like to help others realize the potential of their own vision in their own communities. It goes back to the franchising analogy: I don't want to work with people who are happy to play by my rules. I'm excited by people who want to do it *better*.

With this in mind, we find it very important to base this on leadership *teams,* not on individuals. There's a tendency in the nonprofit world to identify a hero in every organization—one person who is changing the world. And that is bullshit. For every visionary leader, there are dozens of hardworking, extraordinarily dedicated, exceptionally talented people putting that vision into action. Sure, the vision is important, but a vision is worth nothing without execution.

So our plan involves finding teams of people working in community development and helping to create a pathway for them to structure their organizations, support leadership and staff development, and build networks with other community workers.

It can be hard to take a step back and think about these issues when you are still in the heart of the community you are working in, and even more difficult to access leaders and innovators from both the nonprofit and other industries who can offer new ways of thinking about the world. As much as I complain about the conference circuit, these gatherings provide a chance to cross-pollinate ideas, to hear from Jack Ma, the founder of Alibaba, weeks after going public, on the journey from building Web sites in his living room to having the largest IPO ever, or from Paul Farmer on how we should address Ebola. A few years ago, I was seated next to Tim Berners-Lee, the founder of the World Wide Web, at a breakfast meeting during the Decide Now Act Summit. Across the table was Bob Geldof, the legendary founder of the philanthropic group Band Aid. It was awe-inspiring and invigorating to be able to be in the presence of and to listen to these people who had changed the world, who had connected people in ways that were revolutionary and unimaginable and solved problems that no one else could.

With the Ubuntu Institute, we want to create the opportunity for this type of exposure and this kind of intellectual stimulation.

We think about it as experiential learning: Leadership teams will travel to New York for meetings and training sessions, and then return to their communities to put that knowledge into practice. This allows the teams to get some perspective on their own work, to forge a global network with teams from other regions, and to use the many valuable resources that exist in New York, from development experts to donors, whom they might otherwise never get the opportunity to access—all while still being intimately involved on the ground in their own communities. Each team will have a dedicated mentor who will work closely with them to provide advice and help develop strategic goals. In the second year, we'll come to the organization's community, to help build a support network around the leadership team in situ.

I think about Karim Abouelnaga, a young man from New York City I'm currently mentoring. Karim started Practice Makes Perfect, an organization that has set out to fill the gap in learning, which often occurs for disadvantaged students during summer break, by creating six-week enrichment programming. We talk regularly about fashioning systems, developing a board, taking care of staff and himself. After all these conversations, I think, *If someone had sat down with me and had these conversations ten years ago, where would Ubuntu be now?*

Those conversations, those relationships, make a meaningful difference to leadership teams and to organizations. Karim has access to me; he's had the opportunity to work with the Clinton Global Initiative University, a meeting for university-age social entrepreneurs; he sees peers taking on similar initiatives—none of this was around when Banks and I started Ubuntu. These make it a little easier for Karim: He has a ready community to turn to.

But there's still no organization that focuses solely on mentorship and capacity building for grassroots leadership teams specifically. That's the void that the Ubuntu Institute wants to fill.

Ubuntu has never shied away from risk, and we've never hesitated to forge our own path. We want to extend our impact, but to do it in a way that feels organic to our organization; we have no interest in expanding for expansion's sake. Most important, we don't want to detract from our work in Port Elizabeth. Ubuntu Education Fund will run in the way it always has: with focus, with flexibility, with best practices, and with innovation. The Ubuntu Institute will allow us to fulfill our obligation as people who care about development, who believe in fighting poverty and its root causes, who want to change the world, and to do so in the spirit of *ubuntu* that has always guided us. Imagine what could happen after five years: Twenty-five sites around the world that have had the chance to use our years of experience to fast-forward their own development. That's what scale looks like to me.

ACKNOWLEDGMENTS

Ubuntu Education Fund is about a collective: the employees, board members, donors, and volunteers, and a global network of supporters who make what we do possible. Over the years, many people have contributed to our evolution. This is a story about people buying into a vision early on and not leaving it, of dedication, of commitment, of putting a team together. We call it the Ubuntu family. And to that Ubuntu family: Thank you.

Special thanks are due to Banks, for letting me into your life and showing me the true spirit of *ubuntu*; to Stephanie Tade for believing in this project and supporting us throughout the process; and to the amazing Rodale team for making *I Am Because You Are* possible.

REFERENCES

In the course of my years working in South Africa, and while writing this book, many books, articles, and other resources have influenced me.

SOUTH AFRICA AND AFRICA
Books

Coetzee, J. M. *Waiting for the Barbarians*. New York: Penguin Books, 1982.

Hochschild, Adam. *King Leopold's Ghost: A Story of Greed, Terror, and Heroism in Colonial Africa*. Boston: Mariner Books, 1999.

Krog, Antjie. *Country of My Skull: Guilt, Sorrow, and the Limits of Forgiveness in the New South Africa*. New York: Broadway Books, 2000.

Malan, Rian. *My Traitor's Heart: A South African Exile Returns to Face His Country, His Tribe, and His Conscience*. New York: Grove Press, 1990.

Mandela, Nelson. *Long Walk to Freedom*. New York: Little, Brown, 1994.

Mathabane, Mark. *Kaffir Boy: The True Story of a Black Youth's Coming of Age in Apartheid South Africa*. New York: Free Press, 1998.

Mda, Zakes. *The Madonna of Excelsior*. New York: Farrar, Straus, and Giroux, 2004.

Russell, Alec. *Bring Me My Machine Gun: The Battle for the Soul of South Africa, from Mandela to Zuma*. New York: PublicAffairs, 2009.

Sparks, Allister. *Beyond the Miracle: Inside the New South Africa*. Chicago: University of Chicago Press, 2003.

———. *The Mind of South Africa*. New York: Alfred A. Knopf, 1990.

———. *Tomorrow Is Another Country: The Inside Story of South Africa's Road to Change*. Chicago: University of Chicago Press, 1996.

Tutu, Desmond. *No Future without Forgiveness*. New York: Doubleday, 1999.

Articles

Dugger, Celia W. "Eager Students Fall Prey to Apartheid's Legacy," *New York Times,* September 19, 2009.

Goldsmith, Arthur A. "Foreign Aid and Statehood in Africa," *International Organization* 55(1): 123–48, 2001.

Keller, Bill. "Walter Sisulu, Mandela Mentor, and Comrade, Dies at 90," *New York Times,* May 6, 2003.

Power, Samantha. "The AIDS Rebel," *The New Yorker,* May 19, 2003.

Roeder, Amy. "The Cost of South Africa's Misguided AIDS Policies," *Harvard Public Health*, Spring 2009. *hsph.harvard.edu/news/magazine/spr09aids*

Specter, Michael. "The Denialists," *The New Yorker,* March 12, 2007.

Theroux, Paul. "Africa's Aid Mess," *Barron's,* November 30, 2013.

Online Resources

The Cradock Four: *thecradockfour.co.za*

South African History Archive: *saha.org.za*

Truth and Reconciliation Commission hearings transcripts: *justice.gov.za/trc /hrvtrans/*

Truth and Reconciliation Commission coverage by SABC: *sabctrc.saha.org.za*

UNAIDS, the Joint United Nations Programme on HIV/AIDS: *unaids.org/en*

DEVELOPMENT
Books

Easterly, William. *The White Man's Burden: Why the West's Efforts to Aid the Rest Have Done So Much Ill and So Little Good.* New York: Penguin Books, 2006.

Kamkwamba, William and Bryan Mealer. *The Boy Who Harnessed the Wind: Creating Currents of Electricity and Hope.* New York: William Morrow, 2009.

Kidder, Tracy. *Mountains beyond Mountains: The Quest of Dr. Paul Farmer, a Man Who Would Cure the World*. New York: Random House, 2003.

Moyo, Dambisa. *Dead Aid: Why Aid Is Not Working and How There Is a Better Way for Africa*. New York: Farrar, Straus, and Giroux, 2009.

Novogratz, Jacqueline. *The Blue Sweater: Bridging the Gap between Rich and Poor in an Interconnected World*. New York: Rodale Books, 2010.

Sachs, Jeffrey D. *The End of Poverty: Economic Possibilities for Our Time*. New York: Penguin Books, 2006.

Tough, Paul. *Whatever It Takes: Geoffrey Canada's Quest to Change Harlem and America*. Boston: Mariner Books, 2009.

Articles

Brest, Paul and Kelly Born. "When Can Impact Investing Create Real Impact?" *Stanford Social Innovation Review*, Fall 2013.

Buffett, Warren. "2013 Annual Letter to Berkshire Hathaway Shareholders." February 28, 2014. *berkshirehathaway.com/letters/2013ltr.pdf*

Eckhart Queenan, Jeri, Jacob Allen, and Jari Tuomala. "Stop Starving Scale: Unlocking the Potential of Global NGOs." Boston: Bridgespan Group, April 2013.

Goggins Gregory, Ann and Don Howard. "The Nonprofit Starvation Cycle." *Stanford Social Innovation Review*, Fall 2009.

Marks, Howard. "Annual Memo to Oaktree Clients: Dare to Be Great II." April 8, 2014. *oaktreecapital.com/MemoTree/Dare%20to%20Be%20Great%20II.pdf*

Pallotta, Dan. "The Way We Think about Charity Is Dead Wrong," TED2013, March. *ted.com/talks/dan_pallotta_the_way_we_think_about_charity_is_dead_wrong*

Ruvinsky, Jessica. "The Emotions of Aid." *Stanford Social Innovation Review*, Summer 2011.

Shore, Bill, Darell Hammond, and Amy Celep. "When Good Is Not Good Enough," *Stanford Social Innovation Review*, Fall 2013.

Singer, Peter. "The Why and How of Effective Altruism," TED2013, May. *ted.com/talks/peter_singer_the_why_and_how_of_effective_altruism*

Online Resources

Aspen Global Leadership Network: *aspeninstitute.org/leadership*

Clinton Global Initiative: *clintonfoundation.org/clinton-global-initiative*

Devex: *devex.com/en*

Bill and Melinda Gates Foundation: *gatesfoundation.org*

The Guardian Global Development: *theguardian.com/global-development*

A View from the Cave: *aviewfromthecave.com*

Skoll World Forum: *skollworldforum.org*

Stanford Social Innovation Review: *ssireview.org*

World Economic Forum: *weforum.org*

UBUNTU EDUCATION FUND

Articles

Field, Stan and Jess Field. "Designing Ubuntu: A Community and Health Centre in South Africa." *http://issuu.com/ubuntueducationfund/docs/designing-ubuntu*

Gerfen, Katie. "2009 P/A Awards: The Ubuntu Center," *Architect*, January 2009.

Online Resources

Ubuntu Education Fund: *ubuntufund.org*

Zethu's speech at the 2007 Clinton Global Initiative midyear meeting: *youtube. com/watch?v=u8ZkUVoxdcc*

Lungi's speech at the 2009 Ubuntu Education Fund gala: *youtube.com/watch ?v=UDANQ7OjaEU*

My TEDxBrooklyn talk, "How Many Kids Can I Get for $10,000?" December 6, 2013: *youtube.com/watch?v=4W5-XeQvOgs*

GLOSSARY

BANTU: *During apartheid, this term came to refer to black South Africans. (The four official racial categories were Bantu, White, Coloured, and Asian, as defined by the Population Registration Act No. 30 of 1950.) Bantustans were created as separate "homelands" for black South Africans and were typically lacking in economic and natural resources.*

BUTHI: *a Xhosa term of respect for a man—any male who has gone to the bush for circumcision.*

BRAAI: *an Afrikaans word meaning "barbecue;" this is a social tradition that transcends the food that is served. Every province, every tribe, every household has its own culture of the braai, from what they put in to how they serve it out. No matter what language you speak, it's still called a braai.*

COMBI: *the most common form of transportation in the townships, these small vans are often overflowing with people, animals, and packages. They're constantly blaring loud bass music out of their speaker systems.*

DAGGA: *slang for marijuana.*

GOGO: *an affectionate Xhosa term for an older woman, something like "Granny."*

INDUKU: *fighting sticks used for sparring matches and often carried as part of young men's circumcision rituals.*

KAFFIR: *a racial slur.*

KWAITO: *a type of music popular in the townships of South Africa, sometimes referred to as "African hip-hop."*

LOXION: *a form of "location," another name for the townships.*

SANGOMA: *a shaman or healer; the term generally encompasses a wide range of traditions across South Africa that draw on ancestral spirits for healing.*

SHEBEEN: *a township bar; these can range from a large commercial establishment to a more informal gathering spot in a neighborhood home. They were illegal under apartheid and now serve as a center of township social life.*

SIS: *short for "sister," South Africans use the term as a sign of respect.*

SPAZA: *a township convenience store, usually run informally out of someone's home.*

TSOTSI: *a township gangster*

UMQOMBOTHI: *a traditional beer made from maize*

ZOL: *slang for a joint*

INDEX

Underscored references indicate boxed text. An asterisk (*) indicates photos in the color inserts.